SCANDINAVIAN COOKING

SCANDINAVIAN COOKING

CLASSIC COOKING FROM SWEDEN, NORWAY, DENMARK AND FINLAND

Sonia Maxwell

THE
APPLE
PRESS

A QUINTET BOOK

Published by The Apple Press
6 Blundell Street
London N7 9BH

ISBN 1-85076-569-3

This book was designed and produced by
Quintet Publishing Limited
6 Blundell Street
London N7 9BH

Creative Director: Richard Dewing
Designer: Ian Hunt
Managing Editor: Helen Denholm
Editor: Barbara Croxford
Photographer: Nick Bailey

Picture credits
The publishers would like to thank the following
organizations for supplying pictures of Scandinavia.
Danish Tourist Board: pages 1 (D. Betz), 13 (O.
Akhof), 51 (D. Betz), 77 (D. Betz), 113 (Mayher)
Finnish Tourist Board: pages 7, 12, 18, 31, 66
Life File: pages 6 (Cecilia Innes), 10 (Nigel
Shuttleworth), 21 (Richard Powers), 65 (Eric Wilkins),
75 (Cecilia Innes), 79 (F. Ralston), 111 (Andrew
Ward), 121 (Terry O'Brien)
Norwegian Tourist Board: pages 9, 33, 82, 95
Swedish Travel and Tourism Council: pages 11
(Göran Assner), 54 (Per Klaesson)

Typeset in Great Britain by
Central Southern Typesetters, Eastbourne
Manufactured in Singapore by
Bright Arts (Singapore) Pte. Ltd.
Printed in Singapore by
Star Standard Pte. Ltd.

CONTENTS

SCANDINAVIA – LAND OF THE MIDNIGHT SUN

Sweden, Finland, Norway and Denmark form the most northerly region of Europe, Scandinavia – a region which has seen many political alliances: Sweden united with Norway and Denmark; Sweden with Finland; Denmark with Norway. So it is easy to understand the influence each of these countries has had upon its neighbours. Their shared traditions, customs and cuisines can be traced back to the Vikings. However, they are four quite independent countries, each of which has retained unique and unmistakable characteristics.

The people of the north are as different from each other as the lands in which they dwell, but they share a love of nature. The great distances which separate communities in the sparsely populated countryside of Sweden, Norway and Finland, and the 150,000 lakes which break up Sweden's land mass, have also given the people a taste for silence and solitude. Forests stretch north to Lapland where they peter out and eventually make way for vast wastelands of ice and snow. The people may seem reserved on first meeting but, once the ice is broken, it is easy to see how they gained their high spirited and easy-going reputation. The need to contend with natural elements has made them excel at sports such as skiing, ice-skating, canoeing, fishing and sailing.

Because of its latitude, Scandinavia's seasonal pattern is unique and it is the hours of daylight rather than the temperature which determine the change of season. In some regions there may be 19 hours of daylight on a summer day and people enjoy the long evenings outdoors: in June and July there is no night in Lapland. Winter brings snow and long hours of darkness and the fireplace is at its most inviting at this time of year. When the sun sets in the depth of winter, it does not rise again for another 51 days.

The Vikings were hospitable people who left a door open for the unexpected guest and hospitality is still a characteristic of Scandinavians today. Scandinavians have also gained a reputation for good design. They spend a great deal of time in their homes and have become expert at furnishing their dwellings comfortably. Their imaginative table settings for entertaining are renowned and it follows that people who take such care in presentation should also care about food. This is illustrated by the attention lavished on the delicacies which make up the Smörgåsbord, one of the better known preparations of the Scandinavian kitchen.

Scandinavian cuisine can be described as complicated, varied and in harmony with nature – the key to the Nordic table being the climate. To survive the long winters, people had to store supplies. As a result every possible method of preservation was used to produce a selection of dried, smoked and cured meat and fish, unmatched anywhere else. The Vikings took these preserves with them on their long voyages to distant lands for sustenance and as a means of bargaining. Local produce has always formed the basis of Scandinavian cuisine and game is used extensively (bear, reindeer, elk, snow grouse and snow hare). The sea is also a great provider and crayfish, lobster, oysters, mussels, herrings, trout, salmon and cod are abundant.

The lavish interior of the Stockholm Opera café.

When salt was too expensive or in short supply, other means of preserving had to be found – meat would be stored in butter or whey and fish was sometimes buried in a crude attempt at refrigeration. The fish often fermented and this was considered a delicacy. Swedish Surstromming, a Baltic herring preparation based on this practice, is one dish which still survives today.

But salt has always been a favourite condiment and, in times gone by, when the price of salt dropped and people found it once again affordable they would use it with such zeal in the preservation of food that violent thirsts were commonplace. Although salt is no longer used so liberally, Scandinavians still have a taste for salty foods. Many recipes use fresh meat which has been boiled in brine and left to soak for days to impart flavour and tenderize it.

Herring and cod are hung up and left to dry in the brisk Atlantic wind. Dried cod, known as "stokkfisk", is later made into "lutefisk" by soaking it in a lye (alkaline) solution before cooking. Because cod and herring are so readily available and so easily preserved, they have become two of Scandinavia's principal sources of food, and major exports. Dried and salt cod preparations introduced to Portugal, Spain and Italy by the Vikings during their voyages to Southern Europe have remained popular in these countries.

Smoking houses provided a wide range of smoked meats and fish for the Scandinavian table but the Vikings also savoured mutton, cabbage, apples, cheese, cucumber, horseradish, mushrooms, nuts and berries – all of which continue to feature in the Scandinavian diet. Parsley and dill in particular are used extensively to flavour and garnish dishes. Other staple foods include a variety of cultured milks (fresh milk is a popular drink), fresh and soured cream and salted butter. The range of crispbreads and flatbreads available is as wide as that of leavened bread. Moisture content of crispbreads and flatbreads is low in order to ensure good keeping qualities and some have a hole in the centre so they can be hung from the rafter to keep them dry.

Scandinavians like to precede or accompany their food with the strong liqueur, Aquavit, and beer. Norwegian beer is good and much enjoyed in Norway – it is also exported to the United States. Beers range from strong "Easter" beers (8 per cent alcohol) to lighter varieties to quench a summer thirst. Although Aquavit is enjoyed throughout Scandinavia, each nation has its favourite ritual or particular way of serving the liqueur. The Danes like a strong, piping hot coffee with Aquavit. It can also be served in chilled, long-stemmed glasses and downed in one. A

The sea is an important provider of fish for all the Scandinavian countries.

toast in Aquavit is a solemn procedure, involving looking your companion in the eye, saying "Skal", and emptying your glass in one. Aquavit is not the only spirit enjoyed in Scandinavia, scotch and gin are popular in Norway and, with Russia on their eastern border, it is not surprising that the Finns like vodka.

Fresh garden produce, salads, berries, fruits, fresh fish, often plump with roe, and creamy dairy products are the foods of summer when most meals are eaten outdoors to take full advantage of the long daylight hours. As winter closes in, people turn to their cosy, comfortable homes and flickering candlelight adds warmth and colour. Game and mushrooms from the forest, simmering stews and home-baked breads grace the table as the days become shorter.

To delve into Scandinavian cuisine is to take a journey through its countryside and perhaps to catch a glimpse of its people. Dishes vary with the region but each has a special significance and perhaps a story to tell.

SCANDINAVIA

NORWAY

The scenery in Norway can only be described as dramatic. It is a land of high, snow-capped mountains, fjords cut deep into the coastline and virgin forest teeming with wildlife. Here you can only marvel at the toughness of a land where only 4 per cent of the ground can be cultivated.

Norwegians love the outdoor life and retreat to their "hytter" or cabins to escape from the stress of modern times. Here they hunt, fish, pick wild berries and mushrooms, and enjoy nature's bounty. They are a resilient people who enjoy hiking in summer and skiing in winter. However, they retain a healthy respect for the mountainous landscape, leaving vast areas of the country in a virgin state.

Norwegians are proud of their Viking ancestors who first united the country in the 8th century, but for the next thousand years the country was under the rule of either Denmark or Sweden. Full independence was only achieved in 1905, despite the fact that the constitution was written in 1814. The 19th century produced many of Norway's great names – the composer Edvard Grieg, dramatist Henrik Ibsen, artist Edvard Munch and polar explorer Roald Amundsen among them.

Winters are relatively mild along the coast, particularly in the south of the country – the Gulf Stream usually keeps the temperature in Oslo no lower than –8°C/20°F. Inland and further north it is a different story – winters are long, very cold and very dark. Summers are mild but the temperature can drop sharply at night.

Due to the need to keep out the cold, Norwegians have long regarded food as fuel. Breakfast tends to be substantial with herring, cold meats and cheese served with crusty bread. Lunch breaks are short and the midday meal often consists of open sandwiches so the hot meal of the day is eaten early, around 4 or 5 o'clock.

Norway extends more than 1,500 miles from north to south, so it comes as no surprise that diets vary widely. Shellfish are popular in the south, while whalemeat is considered a delicacy in the north. Crystal clear rivers provide a wealth of freshwater fish, including the noble salmon, and fish dishes are a speciality of Norwegian cuisine. Sheep and goats adapt more easily to the mountainous country than cattle, and game is always popular. Fish and meat are often preserved for consumption during the long, dark winters, especially in the Northern islands. Fish is dried in the ice cold winds, while mutton is salted or smoked first.

Norway was a poor country until the '50s, trading mostly in fish and timber and with little industrialization. Then, in 1968, came the discovery of oil in the North Sea which reversed Norway's fortunes and in its wake brought Norwegians one of the world's highest standards of living. Today Norway is modern and highly industrialized, but nature still dominates vast areas of virgin land, allowing its people to enjoy both the benefits of a wealthy nation and the rare pleasures of the simple life.

Children in national costume from Finmark –
the northernmost part of Scandinavia.

DENMARK

The geographical position of the Danish peninsular and its numerous islands (there are some 450 of them) form a link between Europe and Scandinavia. In contrast to other Scandinavian countries, Denmark's landscape is flat or gently undulating and the climate, tempered by the Gulf Stream, is warm in summer but wet and grey with little snow in winter.

In the country's 17,018 square miles, live 5 million Danes; a peace-loving people who take pride in their efficient, state-funded social welfare system and in their high standard of living. But it was not always so. Jylland (Jutland) was inhabited by nomadic hunters until, in AD500, a tribe from Sweden moved south. The tribe was known as "Danes". The land they moved to became Denmark.

The country's strategic position and Viking expansionism led to many struggles with England and Western Europe for control of the North Sea, with Norway and Sweden for the straits between Denmark and Norway, and with Germany, Poland and Russia for the Baltic.

The Vikings were skilled and daring seafarers with swift, seaworthy ships – a big advantage in their many voyages and successful raids. They occupied much of England and Ireland, and continued south along the coast of France, on to Sicily and as far as the Black Sea. To the north their voyages took them to Iceland, Greenland and Canada.

As Europe learned to defend its territories, Viking dominance receded. By the 18th century, Denmark had become a democracy and its energies were turned towards cultural pursuits.

The principal islands of Denmark differ widely in character. The statue of the Little Mermaid is a well-known landmark is cosmopolitan Copenhagen on the island of

The famous Legoland town in Denmark.

Zealand. The capital's Tivoli Gardens is a bustling centre of entertainment and in the north of the island is Hamlet's Kronborg Castle. Fyn was the home of Hans Christian Andersen and this island's rich farmlands have earned it a reputation as the granary of Denmark. Fruit comes from the orchards of Lolland and Falster, and here too amber is found and made into jewellery. Many Stone Age monuments are to be found on the island of Mon, which is also distinguished by 12th and 13th century village churches, decorated with frescos depicting Biblical scenes.

Bornholm is Denmark's holiday island 88 miles east of the mainland. Golden fields, prosperous farms and forests mirror the Danish landscape in miniature, and old village inns provide warm hospitality.

Fish is the principal export of the Faroe Islands (there are 18 of them) which are also renowned for their knitwear.

Danes love good food and need little encouragement to stop for coffee and a Danish pastry or a Danish open sandwich (Smørrebrød) between meals. Local cooking combines wholesome country fare with the refinement of aristocratic culinary skills which were themselves influenced by foreign lands and French cuisine in particular.

Danes eat more meat than other Scandinavians. Home-produced pork, hams and bacon are favourites. Small game, such as hare and pheasant, are also popular and chicken is traditional on Sundays. Fish and Denmark's wide assortment of cheeses also feature very prominently on the menu.

Fertile, mild Denmark is Scandinavia's "land of milk and honey" where the scenery, culture and food of north and south meet and mix to the benefit of all.

SWEDEN

Look at the map of Sweden and you begin to grasp the size of this vast Scandinavian country. Sweden stretches almost 1,000 miles from its barren, arctic northern tip to its fertile south. It is the fourth largest country in Europe but its population has remained relatively small (8.5 million) and thinly spread. It is a country of staggering contrasts with vast forests covering 50 per cent of the land, innumerable lakes including two of the largest in Europe, desolate moorland and rushing rivers. Although relatively flat or gently rolling for the most part, the land mass is broken by a mountain range in the north west with peaks rising to more than 2,000 metres and the coastline is dotted with countless islands which make popular summer retreats.

Elk, reindeer, bear and lynx roam the forests; lakes and rivers are a rich source of fish, while sea eagles and ospreys soar high in the sky.

The climate is one of harsh contrasts with warm summers and long hours of daylight, earning the country its reputation as the land of the midnight sun, followed by bitterly cold, dark winters. Contrasts continue between Sweden's Viking past and its ultra-modern cities; shops filled with the latest designs in goods and fashions highlight Sweden's regard for the traditional skills of woodcarving, weaving and glass blowing. The music of the '40s and '50s is widely heard despite the international reputation of rock groups such as Abba, and sexual liberation is tempered by the high value placed on family life.

Traditional festivals have an important place in the Swedish calendar. Typical of the country's annual celebrations are the Feast of Valborg on April 30, when bonfires are lit to mark the end of winter, and the Midsummer Day festivities when Swedes decorate their homes with garlands of flowers, dance around maypoles and stay up with the sun throughout the night. But perhaps the best-known festival, and one which is said to have its roots in pagan times, is that of the Day of Santa Lucia, Queen of Light, on December 13. Young girls chosen to represent the saint wear a crown of candles in their hair (usually an electric substitute nowadays) and, accompanied by

their handmaidens, they "reign" over the celebrations which mark the beginning of the Christmas season.

Preserving the natural heritage is also high on Sweden's list of priorities and, as a result, fish abound even in the waters of Stockholm city centre and hares have adopted the parks of Malmö!

Stockholm is considered to be one of Europe's most beautiful capital cities. Built on fourteen islands, it is a city of green parks, handsome squares and airy boulevards. It is also a city of contrasts with ultra modern skyscrapers never more than a few minutes walk from medieval streets. Stockholm's efficient infrastructure of roads and railways make it possible for Stockholmers to live in the suburbs built in the pine forests and by the lakesides around the capital. Sweden is rich in natural resources. In addition to a thriving industry in pulp, paper and wood products (60 per cent of which go to export), natural resources include uranium, iron ore and other metals. Hydroelectric plants account for some 15 per cent of energy supplies and this cheap source of power has played a major part in Sweden's industrial development.

Swedish cooking is wholesome and tasty. The laden Smörgåsbord table is perhaps the most widely known of their delicacies. Every housewife takes great pride in the preparation of this meal which consists of a selection of delicacies served buffet style. The origin of the Smörgåsbord is said to go back more than 200 years when it was the traditional meal of country people.

Fish (fresh, smoked or pickled) is a speciality and herring is a particular favourite. In season, hunting is popular, adding elk, venison, hare and all types of game to the cuisine. Autumn brings an exotic variety of

A typical Swedish harbour, with wooden houses bordering the water's edge.

mushrooms and fruits, such as blackberries, blueberries and cranberries, with the country's rich dairy products forming the basis of delicious pastries and delicious creamy desserts.

Sweden is often described as a "rich" country, a fact reflected in the wealth of its natural resources, the abundance of its wildlife and the quality of life enjoyed and carefully protected by its people.

FINLAND

*A team of huskies pulling a sledge over the
snowbound landscape of Finland.*

The culture and the way of life of the people of Finland is unique – even in Scandinavia. The population is spread far and wide across the land and their culture is closely linked to nature – not surprising since the forest is everywhere, even in the heart of the capital, Helsinki. The extensive moorlands and swamps of southern and central Finland are interspersed with forest and lakes, while the north gradually makes way to tundra where moss and lichen replace fir trees and dense forest vegetation.

Finnish handicrafts are also quite distinctive from those of other nordic nations. Utensils have been hand made for centuries and carving skills passed on from one generation to the next in isolated villages. The children begin to learn the craft at an early age, devoting much of their life to perfecting the skill.

Strictly speaking, Finns are not Scandinavian and their native tongue is a link with their distant past. Their ancestors came from central Asia and moved north to settle on the swampy shores of the Gulf of Finland, displacing the Lapps who moved further north still, into Lapland.

Sweden and Russia fought over Finland for centuries and, after more than 600 years under Swedish rule and 100 under the czars of Russia, it is inevitable that Finland should bear traces of their two cultures.

One third of Finland lies north of the Arctic Circle and although temperatures here can drop to –30°C (–20°F) in winter, the effect of the Gulf Stream makes it the warmest of the Scandinavian countries in summer when temperatures are often over 20°C (68°F). The winter months (mid-November to February) are cold and dark. Summer is short but very light – in the extreme north the sun doesn't set at all during June and July – and it is in this brief period that crops are grown.

Gratins and stews are popular in Finland and a gratin of swede, a favourite vegetable, is a traditional Christmas Day dish. Breads range from flatbreads and crispbreads (mainly in the west and reflecting the influence of Sweden) to sourdough rye (typical in the east and also found in Russia and central Europe). Fish stews are an economical way of utilizing the heat left over after baking. Thick gruels and porridges are popular, made from different grains and topped with berry purées or cream. The Finns produce their own version of the Swedish Smörgåsbord but their cuisine also reflects the borscht soup and meat kebabs of neighbouring Russia.

Although the food of Finland reflects the influence of its neighbours, both east and west, it is based on the produce of its land. Finns see the fruits and wildlife of nature as a gift to be cherished. Their calm approach to life is a result of their love of the nature which surrounds them.

1

SOUPS

SUMMER VEGETABLE SOUP
KESAKEITTO

Made from summer vegetables picked at their absolute peak of freshness, this is a light, healthy soup. It is a favourite for a lunch or a late supper. The meal is often finished with small pancakes and jam.

SERVES 6–8

4 small carrots	2 tbsp plain flour
175g/6oz peas	100ml/4fl oz milk
1 small cauliflower	1 egg yolk
2 new potatoes	50 ml/2fl oz double cream
225g/8oz string beans	225g/8oz small peeled prawns
4 small radishes, halved	1 tsp white pepper
100g/4oz fresh spinach, washed	2 tbsp finely chopped fresh dill
2 tsp salt	or parsley
25g/1oz butter	

Prepare and cut the vegetables into 8mm/¼in cubes, except for the peas and spinach. Place the cubed vegetables and peas in a saucepan, cover with cold water and add the salt. Boil, uncovered, for 5 minutes or until tender. Add the spinach and cook for another 5 minutes. Strain the liquid into a bowl and put the vegetables into another bowl.

Melt the butter, remove from the heat and stir in the flour. Slowly add the hot vegetable stock, whisking all the time, then beat in the milk. Mix the egg yolk and cream in a small bowl. Whisk 150ml/¼pt of the hot soup into the egg mixture, spooning it in. Then whisk the warmed egg and cream mixture back into the soup.

Add the vegetables to the soup and reheat. Just before it boils, add the prawns and simmer for 3–4 minutes. Season to taste. Serve with chopped dill or parsley.

BEER SOUP

ØLLEBRØD

SERVES 4–6

8 slices of pumpernickel
600ml/1pt dark malt beer
  or brown ale
225ml/8fl oz water
grated rind and juice of 1 lemon
sugar, to taste
150ml/¼pt whipped cream

This very popular Danish soup, rarely tasted by foreigners, should be as thick as porridge. A sweet dark, non-alcoholic malt beer is traditionally used.

Cut the bread into small pieces and place in a deep dish. Pour the beer and water over the bread and leave to soak for a minimum of 3 hours.

    Transfer the mixture to a saucepan and simmer over a low heat until it thickens to the desired consistency. Purée in a food processor at medium speed. Add the lemon rind and juice and sweeten with sugar to taste. Return to the heat and bring to the boil. Serve hot with whipped cream.

FINE FISH SOUP

FIN FISKESUPPE

SERVES 4–6

1 kg/2lb turbot or brill
1 litre/1¾pt water
2 tsp salt
3–4 peppercorns
1 medium onion, sliced
1 carrot
1 leek
1 green pepper
1 small can pimento
50ml/2fl oz oil
15g/½oz butter
½ tsp curry powder
1 clove garlic, crushed
150–200ml/¼–⅓pt white wine
salt and pepper

All the flavour of fish and fresh vegetables plus a tang of garlic and spices makes this a fine soup.

Clean and fillet the fish. To make the stock, discard the gills, then put the fish head, skin and bones in a saucepan with the water, the salt, peppercorns and onion. Bring to the boil, reduce the heat and simmer the stock for about 30 minutes, then strain it. Cut the fish fillets into narrow pieces and simmer in some of the fish stock for 5–10 minutes.

    Prepare and cut the vegetables into fine strips. Cook in the oil and butter with the curry powder and garlic until all the vegetables are tender. Add the wine and boil for a few minutes. Add the fish stock and simmer the soup until the vegetables are tender. Add the fish and heat through thoroughly. Season to taste.

NETTLE SOUP

NÄSSELSOPPA

SERVES 4–6

225g/8oz fresh young nettles

salt and pepper

5 tbsp chopped fresh chives

25g/1oz butter

3 tbsp plain flour

1.2–1.5 litres/2–2½pt beef stock

All that is needed for this first taste of spring is a carrier bag and a pair of gloves for picking those young, tender shoots while out on your spring walk. For colour, add hard-boiled eggs, prawns and croûtons.

Rinse the nettles thoroughly in cold water. Boil them for about 15 minutes until tender in lightly salted water. Drain and finely chop the nettles with the chives.

Melt the butter, add the flour and cook for 2–3 minutes, stirring continuously. When golden brown, add the beef stock and boil for 10 minutes. Add the nettles and chives to the soup. Season with salt and pepper. If liked, serve with a poached egg or half a hard-boiled egg per person.

YELLOW PEA SOUP WITH PORK

GUL ÄRTSOPPA MED FLÄSK

SERVES 4–6

425g/15oz dried yellow peas

2 litres/3½pt water

350g/12oz lightly smoked pork, soaked overnight

1 small onion or leek, chopped

½ tsp dried marjoram

salt and pepper

A wholesome soup and almost a meal in itself on a cold day. The smoky flavour of the meat combines well with the yellow peas, and marjoram adds piquancy.

Rinse and soak the peas in the cold water for 10 hours. Cook the peas in fresh water. Bring to the boil quickly and remove any floating pea shells. Put the lid on and repeat the process a few times until most of the floating shells are removed.

Add the pork to the peas with the onion and marjoram. Cover and simmer for about 2 hours. Remove the pork and cut into small pieces. Return the pork pieces to the soup. Season to taste. Serve hot with mustard.

CREME SAINT-GERMAIN

GRÖN SOPPA

SERVES 4–6

1 medium onion, sliced

15–25g/½–1oz butter or
    margarine

1 litre/1¾pt veal or chicken stock

300g/11oz fresh peas or
    1 small can and 1 small packet
    frozen peas

1 tbsp plain flour

1–2 tbsp brandy or Madeira

salt and pepper

1 egg yolk

100ml/4fl oz single cream

HORSERADISH CREAM

150ml/¼pt double cream

2–2½ tsp grated horseradish

CHEESE CROÛTONS

200g/7oz plain flour

100g/4oz Swiss cheese, grated

pinch of salt

100g/4oz butter or margarine

2 tbsp ice cold water

1 egg for glazing

One of the classic soups with a mild, delicate flavour, which gets a kick from the horseradish cream.

Fry the onion in a little of the butter or margarine, without browning. Pour in the stock and add the peas. Boil the mixture for 15 minutes. Blend in a food processor, then strain.

Melt 15g/½oz butter or margarine and stir in the flour. Cook for 2–3 minutes, stirring. Gradually add the strained soup and stir in the brandy or wine and season to taste.

Whisk together the egg yolk and cream in a soup terrine and pour in the soup, stirring vigorously. Serve the soup in heated bowls garnished with a swirl of horseradish cream and cheese croûtons. To make the horseradish cream, simply mix the cream and grated horseradish together.

For the croûtons, mix the flour, cheese and salt together. Crumble the margarine or butter into the mixture. Add the water and quickly mix the pastry together into a ball. Let the pastry rest in a cool place for 30 minutes.

Preheat the oven to 240°C/475°F/Gas Mark 9. Roll out the pastry to a thickness of 3–4mm/⅛in and cut out croûtons. Brush with beaten egg and place on a baking sheet. Bake until golden. Serve warm.

*A herd of reindeer graze for scraps of
edible matter in the snow.*

SWEDE SOUP

KÅLROTSUPPE

SERVES 4–6

1 swede

1.5 litres/2½pt beef stock

15g/½oz butter

1 tbsp plain flour

100ml/4fl oz single cream

pinch of salt

pepper

1 tbsp chopped fresh parsley

A good winter soup that is easy to prepare and economical. Adding a touch of cream gives it a silky smooth texture.

Peel and cut the swede into slices. Boil it in the beef stock for about 25 minutes until tender. Remove and press through a sieve or mash finely, reserving the stock.

Melt the butter in a saucepan and mix in the flour. Cook for 2–3 minutes, stirring. Add the stock and swede pulp. Simmer for 10 minutes. Whip the cream in a tureen. Add the soup, stirring slowly. Season, then sprinkle with chopped parsley.

GOOSE GIBLET SOUP

KRAASESUPPE

SERVES 4–6

gizzard, wings, neck, feet and
  heart of a goose

900ml/1½pt water

4 leeks

4 carrots

100g/4oz celery

10ml/2 tsp salt

4 peppercorns

6 medium tart apples

225g/8oz prunes, stoned

50g/2oz sugar

350ml/12fl oz water

100g/4oz butter

50g/2oz flour

1.5 litres/2½pt giblet stock and
  prune and apple juice, mixed

The Danes are very fond of goose and thick nourishing soups. Since they are also very thrifty, the leftovers of a goose are used to make many other meals as well.

Clean the gizzard and peel off the thick membrane. Cut the wings in half and cut the neck into a few pieces. Remove the skin and claws from the feet. Wash the heart. Place all the giblets in a large saucepan with cold water and bring to the boil. Prepare and cut the leeks, carrots and celery into large pieces and add to the giblets. Season with salt and peppercorns. Cover and simmer for about 2½ hours.

Peel, core and slice the apples and combine with the prunes, sugar and water. Boil the fruit until tender. Drain and discard the fruit, saving the liquid.

Drain the meat, reserving the stock. Melt the butter, add the flour and cook for 2–3 minutes, stirring. Gradually stir in the fruit liquid and stock from the meat. When thickened, return to the pan and cook over a low heat for 10 minutes. Serve with dumplings (page 61).

2

APPETIZERS AND SNACKS

Salmon mousse
Lumpfish roe on toast
Glass blowers' herring
Home-made cheese
Open sandwiches
Appetite sandwich
Danish cheese mousse
Blinis
Liver pâté
Filled bread loaf au gratin

SALMON MOUSSE

LAX MOUSSE

SERVES 4

500g/1lb 2oz cooked salmon,
   boned

2½ tbsp lemon juice

1 tsp salt

cayenne pepper

gelatine

100ml/4fl oz hot salmon liquid
   or water

3 tbsp mayonnaise

3 tbsp dill, finely chopped

75ml/3fl oz double cream, whipped

asparagus tips, hard-boiled egg
   quarters, lemon slices and
   sprigs of dill, to garnish

Delicious summer starter and so pretty too. No need to panic before a dinner party either – the mousse can be prepared in advance and turned out just before serving. Individual moulds make an attractive presentation for a very special occasion.

Flake the salmon with a fork. Mix in the lemon juice, salt and a little cayenne pepper. Dissolve the gelatine in the hot salmon liquid or water. Leave to cool. Mix with the flaked salmon. Add the mayonnaise, dill and whipped cream.

Rinse a 25cm/9¾in mould in cold water. Spoon the mousse into the mould or into smaller individual moulds. Refrigerate until set. Turn out and garnish with asparagus tips, hard-boiled egg quarters, lemon slices and dill sprigs.

◀ *Salmon mousse*

LUMPFISH ROE ON TOAST

LÖJROMS TOAST

SERVES 4

4 slices of brown bread (round
   if available)

40–50g/1½–2oz butter

200g/7oz fresh or frozen peeled
   prawns, thawed

8–10 tbsp mayonnaise

a little tomato purée and
   Worcestershire sauce

4 slices of lemon

150–200g/5–7oz lumpfish roe
   or bleak roe

dill, to garnish

A really easy and delicious starter for a party. Inspired by Hamburger Börs, a Stockholm restaurant with a great reputation.

Cut out round shapes from the 4 slices of bread, using a large glass or a cup as a guide. Fry the bread in the butter on both sides, then leave to cool.

Peel and chop the prawns and mix with the mayonnaise. Colour and flavour with some tomato purée and Worcestershire sauce. Spread the mixture on the fried bread, placing a slice of lemon on top. Place the bleak roe or lumpfish roe on top of the lemon. Garnish with dill. Serve this delicious toast freshly made.

GLASS BLOWERS' HERRING

LASIMESTARIN SILLI

SERVES 4–6

4 medium herrings

3 medium red onions, sliced

2 carrots, sliced

MARINADE

300ml/½pt pickling vinegar

300ml/½pt sugar

600ml/1pt water

20 whole allspice

20 white peppercorns

4 bay leaves

Finns spend much of their time outdoors, hence their love of fresh fish. These tasty, spicy herrings are at their best when they have been marinated for a few days.

Gut and clean the herrings, then soak in cold water overnight. Drain and dry the herrings. Cut across in 4–5cm/1½–2in thick slices.

For the marinade, mix the vinegar, sugar, water, allspice, white peppercorns and bay leaves. Bring to the boil, then allow to cool at room temperature.

Put the herrings and vegetables in layers in a glass jar. Pour in enough marinade to cover completely. Refrigerate for at least 24 hours before serving. Serve with boiled new potatoes and brown bread.

Glass blowers' herring ▶

HOME-MADE CHEESE

KOTIJUUSTO

SERVES 4–6

3 eggs, size 5

1.2 litres/2pt buttermilk

3.75 litres/7pt milk

salt

chopped fresh parsley, to garnish

Every community has their own design of mould used for these simple cheeses which are often served as a starter on a buffet table.

Whip the eggs and buttermilk until fluffy. Bring the milk to the boil, add the egg mixture and beat well. Switch off the heat and leave the mixture on the hob to cool slowly. (Liquid will form on the top and the cheese will settle on the bottom.)

Line a strainer or cheese mould with muslin. Remove the cheese with a slotted spoon and put it into the lined strainer, sprinkling a little salt in between the layers. Cover with a plate as a weight and refrigerate for 12 hours. Turn out the cheese on to a serving dish and garnish with chopped parsley.

OPEN SANDWICHES

SMØRREBRØD

The open sandwich is the Danish national dish and is enjoyed by everybody. It is said to have been popular with the upper classes as early as the 18th century. The open sandwich is a colourful meal in itself and is eaten with a knife and fork. Cut into quarters, it can be served as a delightful hors d'oeuvres for parties.

Use dark rye bread for open sandwiches; however, if you wish to use white bread, toast it first. The following ideas are suggestions for open sandwiches using all sorts of ingredients.

EGGS AND HERRING

AEGS OG SILD

Spread slices of hard-boiled egg on buttered bread. Place one or more boned herrings lengthwise on the egg. Garnish with cress.

SMOKED SALMON AND SCRAMBLED EGG

ROGET LAKS OG RORAG

Place a piece of smoked salmon on buttered bread. On top of that, diagonally across the bread, spoon a strip of cold scrambled egg. Garnish with finely chopped dill.

ROAST BEEF AND FRIED EGG

BØF MED SPEJLAEG

Place tender slices of cold roast beef on buttered bread. Fry onions until golden and crisp and spread on the slices of beef. Top with fried egg and serve before the egg cools.
Note: Danish eggs are always served sunny side up!

THE HANS ANDERSEN SANDWICH

H.C. ANDERSEN SANDWICH

Butter a piece bread and put two rows of crisp bacon on top. Spread liver pâté across one row of bacon and place tomato slices across the other. Top the tomato with horseradish and a strip of jellied consommé.

COLD ROAST PORK

FLAESKESTEG

Spread thin slices of roast pork on buttered bread. Garnish with crisp pieces of rind (crackling), slices of jellied consommé, cucumber or pickled gherkin and beetroot or red cabbage.

FOR VEGETARIANS

ITALIAN SALAD

ITALIENSK SALAT

Mix together cooked chopped carrots, finely cut asparagus, peas and mayonnaise. Place a lettuce leaf on buttered bread and arrange a thick layer of the Italian salad on top. Garnish with tomato slices and cress. If you are using home-made mayonnaise, add a few drops of tarragon vinegar to the vegetables.

TOMATO WITH RAW ONION

TOMAT MED RAA LOG

Place several slices of tomato on buttered bread. Put a pile of finely chopped raw onion in the centre.

APPETITE SANDWICH

APTITSMÖRGÅS

SERVES 4

4 slices of white or brown bread

1 large onion, finely chopped

8 g /⅓ oz butter

1 can anchovy fillets

1 tbsp chilli sauce

2 tbsp chopped fresh parsley

2 tbsp chopped fresh dill

4 egg yolks

These sandwiches are bound to satisfy most appetites. They are spicy, tasty and full of goodness – a real meal on a slice.

Cut out round shapes from the 4 slices of bread, using a glass or a cup as a guide. Toast the bread. Fry the onion in the butter until soft and golden. Cut the anchovy fillets into small pieces and mix with the onion. Add the chilli sauce, parsley and dill, then quickly fry together.

Divide the mixture between the toasted bread slices. Make a hollow for the egg yolks, then place one yolk on each portion. Serve immediately.

DANISH CHEESE MOUSSE

DANSK OSTEMOUSSE

SERVES 6–8

100g/4oz Samsoe cheese

100g/4oz Danish blue cheese

300ml/½pt double cream

25g/1oz walnuts, chopped

15g/½oz aspic jelly powder

2 tbsp water

2 egg whites

1–2 tsp mustard

1 tsp celery salt (optional)

pepper

sprigs of parsley and glacé
  cherries, to garnish

Denmark is one of the biggest exporters of cheese in the world. Samsoe cheese takes its name from the Danish island of Samsoe. The flavour resembles that of Cheddar. Danish blue has a pleasant, sharp flavour.

Grate both cheeses into a 1.75 litre/3pt bowl. Whip the cream until light and fluffy but not stiff. Stir in the chopped walnuts, then add the mixture to the cheese. Mix the aspic powder and water in a small bowl. Put the bowl in a saucepan of hot water and leave to stand until the powder has dissolved. Leave to cool. Whisk the egg whites until stiff and fold them into the cheese mixture. Season with mustard, celery salt, if using, and pepper. Fold the aspic into the mixture.

Pour the mixture into a 450g/1lb container or mould of your choice. Leave to set in a cool place. Turn out the mousse when required and garnish with sprigs of parsley and glacé cherries. Serve on toast or crackers.

Danish cheese mousse ▶

APPETIZERS AND SNACKS **29**

BLINIS

BLINIES

25g/1oz fresh yeast

150ml/¼pt tepid water

90ml/3½fl oz single cream

150g/5oz plain flour

300g/10oz buckwheat flour

400ml/about 14fl oz hot milk

3 tbsp melted butter

1 tsp salt

2 eggs, size 5, separated

These are classic Russian buckwheat pancakes served with fresh roe, which is seasonal. The finest roe is burbot, which is popular at Christmastime.

Dissolve the yeast in the tepid water. Add the cream and beat in the flours. Leave the batter to stand for 8–12 hours.

Add the hot milk, melted butter and salt, and whisk. Add the egg yolks to the batter, whisking gently. Whisk the egg whites until stiff and fold into the batter, just before frying.

Fry the pancakes gently in a frying pan in the remaining butter for 2–3 minutes on each side. Serve hot with fresh roe, chopped raw onions, freshly ground pepper and soured cream.

LIVER PÂTÉ

MAKSAPASTEIJA

SERVES 4–6

350ml/12fl oz single cream

50g/2oz breadcrumbs

2 medium onions, finely chopped

25g/1oz butter

450g/1lb minced liver (ask the
  butcher to mince the liver twice)

4 tbsp potato flour

1 tbsp sugar

3 tbsp salt

1 tbsp ground ginger

1 tbsp white pepper

2 eggs, size 5, lightly beaten

thin slices of belly of pork or
  streaky bacon rashers

Frequently served as part of the Christmas Eve feast, this liver pâté can be served hot or cold. For a treat, serve with loganberry or cranberry jam or jelly.

Mix the cream and breadcrumbs, then leave to swell. Preheat the oven to 240°C/475°F/Gas Mark 9. Fry the onions in the butter until soft. Leave to cool.

Mix the liver and the rest of the ingredients, except the slices of belly pork, and blend thoroughly. Line a baking dish with the belly of pork. Pour the mixture into the baking dish and cover tightly with foil. Put the dish into a roasting tin of water. Bake for about 2 hours. Refrigerate before serving.

*Christmas is a time of special celebration
in all Scandinavian countries.*

FILLED BREAD LOAF AU GRATIN

GRATINERAD LANDGÅNG

SERVES 4–6

1 small white or brown loaf

100g/4oz smoked sausage

50g/2oz cheese

2 tomatoes

50g/2oz softened butter

1 medium onion chopped

chopped fresh parsley

Gratinerad Landgång makes an unusual but very tasty snack.

Preheat the oven to 240°C/475°F/Gas Mark 9. Slice the loaf but do not cut right through to the bottom. Place the bread on a large piece of foil. Cut the smoked sausage, cheese and tomatoes into cubes. Mix into the butter with the onion and parsley.

Spread the mixture between the slices. Fold up the foil all around the bread. Bake for 15 minutes.

FISH
AND
SHELLFISH

Sandwichgateau with salmon and shellfish

Boiled cod

Parsley sauce

Fish balls

Bornholm omelette

Fish pie

Marinated salmon

Dill and mustard sauce

Tasty fish fillets

Prawns and roe in a bread basket

Curried fish

Oven-roasted pike

Fried Baltic herring with a taste of France

Matjes herring with tomatoes and olives

Fish balls with tomatoes, onion and celery

Fish au gratin

Prawns in dill cream

Smoked salmon with filling

Herring with leek and lemon

Fresh salted salmon

Weiner Christiansen's Singapore eel

SANDWICHGATEAU WITH SALMON AND SHELLFISH
SMÖRGÅSTÅRTA

SERVES 4–6

1 round or oblong white or
  brown loaf, cut into 1½cm/½in
  thick slices

FILLING

6 hard-boiled eggs, chopped
2 x 170g/6oz cans crab meat
100g/4oz smoked salmon
100ml/4fl oz crème fraîche
100g/4oz mayonnaise
3 tbsp finely chopped fresh chives
3 tbsp finely chopped fresh dill
salt and pepper

This delicious sandwichgâteau is filled and covered with smoked salmon and shellfish.

Mix all the ingredients for the filling. Divide it between the layers of bread.

Mix the mayonnaise with the crème fraîche. Do not stir too much. Spread the mixture on top and round the side of the loaf for a smooth finish. Garnish with prawns, folded salmon, roe, cucumber and lemon slices. Cut into portions with a very sharp knife. Serve with a green salad.

GARNISH

100g/4oz mayonnaise	60g/2½oz lumpfish or bleak roe
100ml/4fl oz crème fraîche	½ fresh cucumber, sliced
450g/1lb prawns	slices of lemon
100–200g/4–7oz smoked salmon	

◄ *Sandwichgateau with salmon and shellfish*

BOILED COD
KOGT TORSK

SERVES 4–6

1.5kg/3lb cod
25g/1oz salt
2 tbsp light malt vinegar
1.1 litres/2pt water
chopped fresh parsley, to garnish

It is claimed that Danish fish is so good that you have to go all the way to California to find its equal. This dish is often served on New Year's Eve.

Cut the fish into large pieces. Sprinkle with half of the salt and leave for 10–15 minutes. Rinse the fish thoroughly and place in a saucepan. Add the rest of the salt, the vinegar and the water. Cover and bring the fish gently to the boil. Switch off the heat and leave the fish to stand for about 10 minutes.

Drain the fish. Garnish with chopped parsley. Serve with boiled potatoes, chopped hard-boiled eggs and grated horseradish.

PARSLEY SAUCE

PERSILLESAUS

SERVES 4-6

25g/1oz butter

25g/1oz plain flour

500ml/18fl oz warm fish stock
 or bouillon

2 tbsp finely chopped fresh parsley

salt and pepper

This delicious and simple sauce makes an excellent accompaniment to many plain fish dishes including Fish Balls.

Melt the butter in a pan, add the flour and cook for 2–3 minutes, stirring continuously. Slowly pour in the warm fish stock, stirring all the time. Boil for 10 minutes. Add the parsely and season to taste. Serve with the fish balls.

FISH BALLS

FISKE FARSE

SERVES 4-6

1.25kg/2¾lb fresh fish, minced

salt and white pepper

1 litre/1¾pt fish stock

The delicate flavour of fish is carefully preserved by this gentle way of cooking. The parsley sauce, using fish stock, adds to the flavour of the dish.

Season the minced fish with salt and white pepper. Shape into small round balls. Heat the fish stock in a pan. Put the fish balls into the hot fish stock and simmer gently for 3–5 minutes, until tender. Serve the fish balls with Parsley Sauce (see above), boiled potatoes, green peas and salad.

BORNHOLM OMELETTE

BORNHOLM AEGGEKAGE

SERVES 4-6

6 eggs, size 5

175ml/6fl oz milk or single cream

1 tsp salt

50g/2oz butter

3 small smoked herrings, boned

15–20 radishes

1 head of lettuce

2 tbsp chopped fresh chives

Bornholm is the little paradise island in the Baltic Sea, famous for its unique cliffs, sandy beaches, woods, picturesque little towns and fresh or smoked herring. This unusual omelette has an excellent combination of flavours.

Beat the eggs, milk and salt together. Melt the butter in a frying pan and add the egg mixture. Cook to the desired consistency.

Slice the herrings, radishes, lettuce and chives. Sprinkle on top of the omelette.

Bornholm omelette ▶

FISH PIE

PATAKUKKO

SERVES 4–6

1kg/2lb small perch or vendace

300g/10oz fatty pork, cut
  into strips

1½–2 tbsp salt

DOUGH

200g/7oz rye flour

75ml/3fl oz water

40g/1½oz plain flour

1 tsp salt

A typical dish from Karelia that can easily be carried around. Very good for the lunch box or picnics. The most famous pasty comes from Savo in central Finland called Kalakukko.

Clean the fish and sprinkle with salt. Leave the fish to stand in the refrigerator for a few hours or overnight to allow the salt to soak in. Line a baking dish with strips of the pork. Place the fish in the baking dish and add a drop of water.

   Preheat the oven to 170°C/325°F/Gas Mark 3. Mix together the rye flour, water, plain flour and salt to make the dough. Knead it well on a floured board. Roll out the dough and use to cover the fish in the baking dish. Bake for 2–3 hours until golden.

MARINATED SALMON

GRAVAD LAX

SERVES 4–6

1–1.5kg/2–3lb fresh salmon
  (middle cut)

50g/2oz salt

75g/3oz sugar

plenty of fresh dill

1½ tbsp crushed whole white
  peppercorns

Prepare your own Gravad lax with salmon, trout or mackerel. You would be surprised how easy it is and how delicious. The dill and mustard sauce is a perfect accompaniment.

Ask the fishmonger to fillet the salmon and remove the central bone. Remove any remaining small bones. Mix the salt and sugar together.

   Take a shallow dish and sprinkle with half of the dill. Place one of the salmon fillets on the dill, skin side down. Rub half the mixture of salt and sugar into the salmon. Sprinkle with crushed white peppercorns and half the remaining dill. Repeat the process on the other side of salmon and sandwich together skin side up. Cover with foil.

   Refrigerate for 3 days turning the salmon every 24 hours. To serve, scrape off the seasoning and cut in slices, discarding the skin. Serve with Dill and Mustard Sauce (page 40).

◀ *Marinated salmon*

DILL AND MUSTARD SAUCE

GRAVLAX SÅS

SERVES 4–6

1 tbsp sugar

2tbsp malt vinegar

2 tbsp mild mustard

finely chopped fresh dill

7 tbsp oil

salt and white pepper

As well as accompanying Gravad Lax, this sauce can also be served with other types of fish.

Mix the sugar, vinegar, mustard and dill together. Pour the oil slowly into the mixture, stirring thoroughly. Season with salt and white pepper. Serve with Gravad Lax (page 39).

TASTY FISH FILLETS

FISKEFILETER MED SMAK

SERVES 4–6

6 small tomatoes

1 tsp salt

1 tsp pepper

juice of ½ lemon

100ml/4fl oz dry white wine

1 tbsp finely chopped fresh
    parsley

2 tsp fresh tarragon

700g/1½lb fish fillets, such as
    plaice or whiting

2 tbsp finely chopped onion

SAUCE

200g/7oz fresh or canned
    button mushrooms, sliced

75g/3oz butter

2 tbsp plain flour

200ml/7fl oz fish stock

2 egg yolks

100ml/4fl oz single cream

This recipe gives white fish a colourful new look. Wrapped around a tomato and served on a creamy mushroom sauce, the fillets taste as good as they look.

Scald the tomatoes and sprinkle them with salt and pepper. Mix the lemon juice with the wine, parsley and tarragon. Place the fish fillets in the marinade, sprinkle with salt and pepper, then leave to soak for about 30 minutes.

Preheat the oven to 200°C/400°F/Gas Mark 6. Wrap a fish fillet around each tomato. Sprinkle the finely chopped onion in the base of a buttered ovenproof dish. Place the fish and tomato rolls side by side in the dish. Pour the marinade over. Cover the dish with foil and bake for about 20 minutes.

For the sauce, brown the mushroom slices lightly in the butter. Sprinkle in the flour and cook for 2–3 minutes, then stir in the fish stock and bring to the boil. Mix the egg yolks into the cream. Stir into the sauce; do not boil. Add salt and pepper to taste. Pour some of the sauce into a serving dish and place fish rolls on top. Serve the remaining sauce together with boiled rice.

Tasty fish fillets ▶

PRAWNS AND ROE IN A BREAD BASKET

RÄKOR OCH LÖJROM I TUNNBRÖDSKORG

SERVES 4

100g/4oz peeled fresh prawns

4 tbsp mayonnaise

Italian herb mix

1 bunch of chopped dill

4 slices of thin unleavened bread,
    such as fine matzos

½ iceberg lettuce, chopped

100g/4oz lumpfish or bleak roe

1 lemon, cut into wedges

This dish is easy to make and is much appreciated, as it is colourful and very attractively presented.

Finely chop the prawns. Mix with the mayonnaise and season lightly with Italian herb mix. Add the dill, saving some for garnishing.

To make the bread basket, moisten each piece of bread with water and quickly turn over in a hot, dry frying pan. Lift up the bread slice which is now pliable and place over an inverted glass. Carefully press the bread against glass all round to form a basket. (When the bread has cooled it will be firm and the basket will be ready.)

One third fill the basket with chopped iceberg lettuce. Add the prawn mixture. Shape the roe with a dessertspoon and place on top. Garnish with remaining dill and lemon wedges.

CURRIED FISH

FISK MED CURRY

SERVES 4–6

300ml/½pt water

200ml/7fl oz dry white wine

1 small leek or onion, sliced

5 white peppercorns

1½ tsp salt

500–600g/1–1¼lb white fish
    fillets

boiled long grain rice, to serve

almonds or salted peanuts fried
    in oil, to garnish

This curry sauce is equally good with chicken. Fried almonds add a delicious touch. Lettuce dressed with lemon vinaigrette is a good accompaniment.

Mix the water, wine, leek or onion, peppercorns and salt in a pan. Bring to the boil, cover and simmer for 10 minutes.

Rinse the fish fillets, fold them double and place in a wide saucepan. Strain the liquid and pour onto the fish. Simmer for 6–8 minutes.

For the sauce, melt the butter, add the curry powder and flour, and heat without browning. Add the fish stock gradually, stirring, and simmer for a few minutes. Remove from the heat and whisk in the egg yolk with the cream. Season.

Place the fish on a bed of boiled rice and pour over some of the sauce. Serve the rest separately. Garnish with fried almonds or salted peanuts.

CURRY SAUCE

25g/1oz butter	1 egg yolk
1½ tsp curry powder	100–200ml/4–7fl oz cream
2 tbsp plain flour	salt and pepper
300ml/½pt strained fish stock	

OVEN-ROASTED PIKE

UGNSBAKAD GÄDDA

SERVES 4–6

1kg/2lb pike

2 tsp salt

1 egg, beaten

breadcrumbs for coating

1 tsp ground white pepper

4–6 anchovy fillets

100g/4oz butter, melted

225g/8oz cheese, grated,
   preferably Cheddar or Edam

A very under-estimated fish in England, pike is popular in Sweden. It has a delicious, unusual flavour, well worth exploring.

Preheat the oven to 200°C/400°F/Gas Mark 6. Scale the fish, leave the head on for flavour, but cut off the fins. Rinse and dry. Sprinkle with a little salt and leave for 5 minutes. Turn the fish in the beaten egg, then coat in breadcrumbs mixed with a little white pepper. Arrange the anchovy fillets on top of the fish.

Wrap in foil and bake for 20–30 minutes. Baste with melted butter a few times. Sprinkle with the grated cheese 5 minutes before the end of the cooking time. Serve with steamed vegetables of your choice and boiled potatoes.

FRIED BALTIC HERRING
WITH A TASTE OF FRANCE

STEKT STRÖMMING MED FRANSK DOFT

SERVES 4

1kg/2lb whole herring or
   575g/1¼lb filleted
   Baltic herring

1 tsp salt

7 tbsp breadcrumbs

2 cloves garlic, crushed

½ tsp salt

3 tbsp chopped fresh parsley

2 tbsp chopped fresh thyme and
   rosemary

2 tbsp olive oil

Olive oil, garlic and herbs add a French flavour to this easy and popular herring dish. Fresh sardines may be used instead.

Preheat the oven to 220°C/425°F/Gas Mark 7. Clean and fillet the fish. Sprinkle the flesh side with salt and fold with the skin outwards. Place the fillets in rows in a greased ovenproof dish.

Mix the breadcrumbs, garlic, salt, herbs and olive oil together. Sprinkle the mixture over the herrings. Bake for 20 minutes.

MATJES HERRING
WITH TOMATOES AND OLIVES

TOMATSILL

SERVES 4

2 Matjes herring fillets, canned
  in brine
4–6 shallots or small pickling
  onions
12–14 olives with pimento

MARINADE

200g/7oz tomato ketchup
1 tbsp pickling vinegar
2 tbsp sugar
pinch of salt
1 tsp crushed white pepper
3tbsp oil

*A traditional recipe for herrings in brine with the flavours
imparted by the marinade. The Matjes are a perfect contrast to
plain new potatoes.*

Slice the herring into 5cm/2in strips. Slice the shallots into fine rings.
Layer the herring, shallots and olives in a glass jar.

For the marinade, mix the tomato ketchup, pickling vinegar, sugar,
salt and pepper together. Stir and add the oil slowly. Pour the
marinade over the herring to cover and leave in the refrigerator for a
few hours before serving. Served with new potatoes and brown bread.

Matjes herring with tomatoes and olives ▶

FISH BALLS WITH TOMATOES,
ONION AND CELERY

FISKEBOLLER GRYTE

SERVES 4

700g/1½lb fish balls in stock,
  cooked, see page 36
2 tbsp chopped onion
4 tbsp chopped celery
25g/1oz butter
300g/10oz canned tomatoes
350g/12oz frozen peas
salt and white pepper

*Tasty and different, this fish ball stew is a typical example of
the many Norwegian ways of preparing the abundance of fish
in their waters.*

Allow the fish balls to drain from the stock. Fry the onion and celery in
the butter for a few minutes. Pour in the tomatoes together with their
liquid, then add the peas. Simmer gently until the onion and celery are
soft. Add the fish balls and gently heat through. Season to taste. Serve
with boiled potatoes or rice.

FISH AU GRATIN
FISKEGRATENG

SERVES 4–6

75g/3oz butter

75g/3oz plain flour

400ml/14fl oz milk

3 eggs, separated

½ tsp grated nutmeg

450–750g/1–1½lb boiled white
   fish, such as cod, haddock,
   coley, chopped

salt and pepper

1 tbsp breadcrumbs

melted butter, to serve

A tasty gratin of white fish with a hint of nutmeg. The addition of egg yolks adds a rich flavour and whipped egg whites makes the dish delightfully light.

Preheat the oven to 170°C/325°F/Gas Mark 3. Melt the butter in a saucepan and add the flour. Cook for 2–3 minutes, stirring continuously. Add the milk gradually and bring to the boil. Leave to cool. Stir in the egg yolks, nutmeg, chopped fish, salt and pepper. Finally whisk the egg whites and fold in.

Place the fish mixture in a greased ovenproof dish and sprinkle with the breadcrumbs. Bake for about 1 hour. Serve with melted butter.

PRAWNS IN DILL CREAM
RÄKOR MED DILLGRÄDDE

SERVES 4

400g/14oz peeled prawns

100g/4oz finely chopped dill

300ml/½pt whipping cream

gelatine

2 tbsp sherry

salt and white pepper

finely chopped fresh dill

1 cucumber, sliced

1 lettuce

100g/4oz lumpfish roe

It is always an advantage when food can be prepared in advance for a dinner party. This dish can be served as a starter or for lunch.

Place the prawns in a bowl and add the finely chopped dill. Pour in the cream and place in the refrigerator for a couple of hours.

Dissolve the gelatine in warm water. Drain the prawns from the cream and whisk the cream into the gelatine. Add the sherry and seasoning to taste. Add the prawns to the cream. Pour the mixture into a chilled ring mould and keep in the refrigerator for 5–6 hours until set.

Turn out the prawn ring onto a serving plate. Sprinkle finely chopped dill on top. Garnish with cucumber slices, lettuce leaves and lumpfish roe.

◄ *Prawns in dill cream*

SMOKED SALMON WITH FILLING
RÖKT LAXROS

SERVES 4

4–8 lettuce leaves

150ml/¼ pt whipping cream

15ml/1 tbsp lemon juice

salt and white pepper

3–4 tsp creamed horseradish

350g/12oz fresh prawns peeled,
    or 175g/6oz peeled prawns

8 thin slices of smoked salmon

fresh dill, to garnish

Smoked salmon is delicious served by itself, but filled with prawns and horseradish it is a mouth-watering combination.

Rinse the lettuce leaves and pat dry. Arrange them on a serving plate. Whip the cream, adding the lemon juice, and season to taste. Fold in the creamed horseradish. Add the prawns, saving a few for the garnish.

Spread the prawn mixture onto the salmon slices. Roll them into "roses" and place on top of the lettuce leaves. Garnish the "roses" with prawns and fresh dill.

Smoked salmon with filling ▶

HERRING WITH LEEK AND LEMON
SILL MED PURJOLÖK OCH CITRON

SERVES 4–6

2 salt herrings (4 fillets)

1 leek, cleaned and sliced

1 small bunch of dill, coarsely
    chopped

MARINADE

juice of 2 lemons

2 tbsp pickling vinegar

200ml/7fl oz water

175g/6oz sugar

½ tsp whole allspice

½ tsp white peppercorns

1 bay leaf

The leek and lemon juice add a tangy flavour to the herring – one of the many ways of serving this bountiful fish from the northern waters.

Fillet the salt herrings and soak in water overnight. Mix all the ingredients for the marinade in a saucepan and bring to the boil. Leave to cool.

Slice the herrings into 2.5cm/1in strips. Layer in a glass jar with the sliced leek and dill. When the marinade is cold, pour over enough liquid to cover the herrings. Leave in the refrigerator for 24 hours before serving. Served with boiled new potatoes.

FRESH SALTED SALMON

TOURESUOLATTU LOHI

SERVES 4–6

1 piece middle-cut salmon, about
  1.5kg/3½lb
225g/8oz salt
1 tbsp sugar
3–4 tbsp coarse white pepper
fresh dill

MUSTARD DRESSING

3 tbsp coarse grain mustard
2 tbsp sugar
4tbsp white wine vinegar
175ml/6fl oz olive oil
chopped fresh dill

*A traditional delicacy for the Christmas table which is easy to
prepare. To reach its full flavour, the Finns leave the salmon
outside in the snow for 2–3 days. This dish does not need any
dressing but, if preferred, serve with a coarse mustard dressing.*

Fillet the salmon, leaving the skin on. Wipe the salmon with absorbent
kitchen paper (do not rinse). Sprinkle half the salt into a suitable sized
dish and place one fillet, skin side down, on top. Sprinkle the sugar
and coarse white pepper over both fillets and place the second fillet,
skin side up, on top of the other fillet. Sprinkle the dill and remaining
salt over the salmon.

Cover the dish with foil and put a small weight on top. Keep in a
cool place for 1–3 days. To serve, scrape off all the seasoning and cut
the fillets into diagonal slices.

If liked, serve with mustard dressing. Mix together the mustard,
sugar and vinegar. Add the oil slowly, stirring continuously. Add plenty
of chopped fresh dill.

WEINER CHRISTIANSEN'S
SINGAPORE EEL

SINGAPORE AEL

SERVES 4–6

1.5kg/3lb fresh eel, skinned
50g/2oz butter
2 tbsp mild curry powder
225g/8oz carrots, sliced
225g/8oz celery, sliced
225g/8oz small mushrooms
1 x 400g/14oz can of tomatoes
1 tsp salt
¼ tsp ground black pepper
50ml/2fl oz fish stock or water
225ml/8fl oz dry white wine

*This superb Danish dish is served in many famous restaurants
in Copenhagen. It can also be made with prawns.*

Cut the eel into 4cm/1½in pieces. Heat the butter, stir in the curry
powder and cook over a medium heat for 2 minutes, stirring
constantly. Add all the vegetables. After 2 minutes, add the eel, season,
then stir in the stock and wine. Cover and simmer over a low heat for
20 minutes, stirring occasionally. Serve with rice.

4

MEAT, POULTRY AND GAME

Pork with apples

Raw spiced fillet of beef with spicy sauce

Potato dumplings stuffed with bacon

Ptarmigan (grouse)

Meat loaf en croûte

Braised venison

Meat cakes

Dumplings

Roberto's veal roulades

Karelian stew

Meat balls

Sweetbreads with garlic mayonnaise

Gourmet lamb

Ryypy

Venison with goat's cheese

Summer omelette with sausages

Palace steak

Lamb and cabbage stew

Swedish hash

Meat patties

Easter chicken casserole

Liver and rice casserole

Roast goose

Grouse with cream sauce

Easter veal

Creamed sweetbreads

Fillet of veal à la Oscar

Pigs' trotters

PORK WITH APPLES

SVINEKØD MED
AEBLE

Denmark's favourite meat is pork. The pig in one way or another is the Danes' key export. They have numerous ways of preparing pork but it would be hard to find a more delicious version than this dish.

SERVES 4

450g/1lb streaky bacon rashers
1kg/2lb red eating apples
50g/2oz sugar

Fry the bacon gently and pour off any excess fat into a dish during frying. This will make the bacon nice and crispy. Remove the bacon and keep warm.

Wash, core and slice the apples but do not peel them. Fry the apple slices in a little of the bacon fat until soft. Sprinkle a little sugar over the apples. Place the fried apples and warm bacon rashers in a serving dish. Serve with fried onions or leftovers. This recipe can be used as a topping for open sandwiches.

RAW SPICED FILLET OF BEEF WITH SPICY SAUCE

GRAVAD OXFILE (MED SENAPSÅS)

SERVES 4

about 450g/1lb piece fillet
  of beef
cress, chopped

MARINADE

50ml/2fl oz Madeira
2 tbsp red wine
1 tbsp olive oil
2 tbsp each of crushed white
  peppercorns and allspice
  (or black pepper)
1–2 tsp grated horseradish
  plenty of chopped chives
  or leeks
chopped fresh parsley

SPICY SAUCE

3 tbsp unsweetened mustard
½ tsp sugar
½ tsp salt
1 egg yolk
100–150ml/4–5fl oz oil

Often served with a green salad, without dressing, and bread. Delicious with small bread croûtons scattered on top.

Mix the marinade ingredients together. Place the meat in a shallow bowl and pour the marinade over it. Turn and dab the marinade into the meat. Sprinkle chopped cress over the entire surface. Cover with cling film and refrigerate for 48 hours.

Scrape off the spices and cress. Place the meat in a plastic bag and refrigerate for another 48 hours.

For the sauce, mix all the ingredients together, stirring thoroughly and adding the oil slowly. If required, dilute the sauce with a couple of spoonfuls of water or a little lemon juice.

Slice the beef thinly with a very sharp knife. Serve with the spicy sauce.

Springtime celebrations for young girls in Sweden.

POTATO DUMPLINGS
STUFFED WITH BACON

KROPPKAKOR

SERVES 4–6

12–14 medium potatoes, about
  1 kg/2 lb

2–3 eggs

100–150 g/4–5 oz plain flour

1–1½ tsp salt

2 litres/3½ pt salted water

melted butter, to serve

STUFFING

50–200 g/5–7 oz unsmoked
  bacon, cubed

50–200 g/5–7 oz smoked bacon,
  cubed

2 onions, chopped

½ tsp black pepper

*Potato dumplings with a difference! The salty, smoky taste of
the bacon and onion filling is a delicious surprise inside the
smooth textured dumpling.*

Boil the potatoes until tender, then cool and mash. To make the
stuffing, brown the bacon and onions in a pan. Season with pepper
and cool. Mix the mashed potatoes with the eggs, flour and salt. Knead
into a dough, then shape into a thick roll. Cut into 12–14 slices.

Make a large hollow in each dumpling, fill with the bacon stuffing
and enclose it. Shape into balls and press flat. Bring the salted water to
the boil. Lower the dumplings, a few at a time, into the salted water.
Boil for 5 minutes or until they float to the surface. Serve with melted
butter.

Potato dumplings stuffed with bacon ▶

PTARMIGAN (GROUSE)

RYPER

SERVES 3

3 ptarmigans

3 thin slices of lard or fat bacon

25 g/1 oz butter

salt and pepper

SAUCE

2 tbsp plain flour

300 ml/½ pt stock

1 ptarmigan liver, chopped

100 ml/4 fl oz cream or
  soured cream

50 ml/2 fl oz redcurrant jelly

*Game is a favourite with Norwegians. This method of
preparation keeps the meat moist and succulent. The sharpness
of the redcurrant jelly adds just the right piquancy to the sauce.*

Clean and dry the ptarmigans. Place a slice of lard or fat bacon
underneath the skin of the breast. Truss the ptarmigans as for chicken.
Brown the ptarmigans on all sides in the butter in a pan. Season with
salt and pepper. Pour about 225 ml/8 fl oz boiling water into the pan
and let ptarmigans simmer over a low heat for 45–60 minutes until
tender. Remove the ptarmigans and keep warm.

For the sauce, stir the flour into some cold water. Add to the stock
and simmer for 5 minutes. Add the liver to the sauce. Pour in the
cream and add the redcurrant jelly to taste.

MEAT LOAF EN CROUTE
INBAKAD KÖTTFÄRS

SERVES 4–6

PASTRY

300g/10oz plain flour
225g/8oz butter or margarine
3 tbsp cold water

MINCE

50g/2oz dry breadcrumbs
100ml/4fl oz cream
100ml/4fl oz water
½ onion, chopped
butter for frying
400g/14oz minced beef, veal or
   pork, as available
1½ tsp white pepper

FILLING

100g/4oz frozen chicken livers,
   thawed
½ tsp salt
½ tsp pepper

*The chicken liver filling adds a gourmet touch to the meat loaf.
An attractive dish which tastes as good as it looks.*

For the pastry, mix the butter or margarine into the flour and combine with water to make a dough. Leave in the refrigerator for 1 hour.

Mix the breadcrumbs with the cream and water. Fry the onion in a little butter. Slice the chicken livers, fry and season. Mix the minced meat with salt, pepper, breadcrumb mixture and fried onion. Pat the mixture into a meat loaf shape on moistened greaseproof paper. Cut a line along the top and fill with the livers, then smooth over to cover.

Preheat the oven to 220°C/425°F/Gas Mark 7. Roll out the pastry between sheets of cling film. Remove the cling film now and then to sprinkle with flour. Roll out one rectangle large enough to wrap around the meat loaf. Trim away uneven edges and save for decoration.

Ease the meat loaf on to the pastry. First fold up the short ends, trimming away the pastry at the corners so that it is not too thick. Fold up the long sides but not too tightly. Seal the join. Ease the parcel onto a greased baking sheet. Decorate with pastry trimmings. Bake for 30–35 minutes.

If liked, served with chopped iceberg lettuce and peppers dressed in a mixture of 3 tbsp mayonnaise, 2 tbsp tomato purée, 45ml/3 tbsp water, salt and pepper.

Meat loaf en croute ▶

BRAISED VENISON
PORONKARISTYS

SERVES 4–6

350g/12oz bacon
butter for cooking
1.5kg/3lb venison
1 tbsp salt
10 whole allspice
300ml/½pt water

*In Finland this would be made with reindeer meat, but venison
is just as good. The most common seasonings are green and
black pepper, allspice, bay leaves and salt.*

Cut the bacon into thin strips. Melt the butter in a saucepan and brown the bacon. Cut the venison into thin strips, add a little at a time to the bacon and brown. Add the seasoning and water. Cover and cook slowly for about 30 minutes until tender. Serve with mashed potatoes, cranberries and beer, homemade if possible.

MEAT CAKES
KJOTTKAKER

Ginger and nutmeg gives these meat cakes a distinctive flavour.

SERVES 4

500g/1lb 2oz minced beef

¾ tbsp salt

100g/4oz suet, finely chopped

2 tbsp potato flour or cornflour

400–500ml/14–18fl oz cold
   water or milk

pinch of pepper, ginger and
   grated nutmeg

2 tbsp plain wholemeal flour

50g/2oz butter for frying

500ml/18fl oz boiling water

1 onion

Mix the mince with the salt, suet and potato flour. Stir well in one direction only. Gradually add the cold water or milk until the mix becomes firm in texture. Add all the spices.

Dab each meat cake in flour and fry until brown. Place in a saucepan as they are ready. Add the boiling water and simmer for about 15 minutes. Blanch the onion and cut into slices. Brown, then simmer in the cooking liquid. A sauce may be made by browning butter and flour, gradually adding the cooking water or stock.

Meat cakes ▶

DUMPLINGS
MELBOLLER

Dumplings are a very big part of traditional Danish cooking, especially in the countryside. They are often served with meat as well as in hot or cold soups.

SERVES 4–6

75g/3oz butter
50g/2oz flour
100ml/4fl oz boiling water
2 eggs, size 4 or 5, separated
½ tsp salt
¼ tsp sugar

Melt the butter and stir in the flour, adding the boiling water gradually. Cool the mixture.

Whisk the egg whites until stiff. Add the yolks, salt and sugar to the cold mixture. Fold in the egg whites. Form into small balls. Cook the dumplings slowly in boiling water for a few minutes. Serve with most soups.

ROBERTO'S VEAL ROULADES

ROBERTOS KALVRULADER

SERVES 4

600g/1lb 6oz thick flank of veal, thinly sliced

50g/2oz mushrooms, finely chopped

100g/4oz minced pork

1 tbsp grated parmesan cheese

1 slice of white bread, grated

1 egg, beaten

1 tbsp chopped fresh parsley

1 tsp sage

salt and pepper

butter for cooking

1–2 medium onions, sliced

1 carrot, sliced

300ml/½pt white wine

2 tbsp tomato purée

arrowroot for thickening

This is a traditional Swedish dish. It is as popular in restaurants as it is for dinner parties at home.

Beat the veal slices as thinly as possible and cut in half. Mix together the mushrooms, minced pork, cheese, grated bread, egg, parsley, sage, salt and pepper.

Spread the filling over the veal slices and roll up. Hold the roulades together with cocktail sticks. Brown all over in butter in a frying pan, then transfer them to a flameproof casserole dish. Add the onions and carrot.

Boil the wine and tomato purée in the frying pan and pour into the casserole. Simmer, covered, for 30–40 minutes. Dilute if required with a little warm water. Strain the juices, thicken with a little arrowroot, adjust seasoning and pour back over roulades. Serve with boiled rice or potatoes and a green salad.

Roberto's veal roulades ▶

KARELIAN STEW

KARJALANPAISTI

SERVES 4–6

450g/1lb port

450g/1lb mutton

450g/1lb beef

1½ tbsp salt

15–20 whole allspice

2 onions, sliced

1.1 litres/2pt beef stock

Karelia is eastern Finland and this Karelia stew is an easy start to get acquainted with the eastern flavours. As with all slowly cooked stews, this dish is best cooked a day ahead. Refrigerate and skim off the fat. Reheat in the oven at a medium heat for about 30 minutes until piping hot.

Preheat the oven to 150°C/300°F/Gas Mark 2. Cut the meat into 2.5cm/1in cubes and place in a casserole dish. Add the salt, allspice and onions to the casserole. Add sufficient beef stock to cover the meat. Cook until tender 30–40 minutes, stirring occasionally. Cover the dish with a lid towards the end of the cooking time. Serve with mashed potatoes.

MEAT BALLS
KÖTTBULLAR

SERVES 4–6

7 tbsp breadcrumbs

300ml/½pt cream and water
 mixture

350g/12oz minced beef

100g/4oz minced veal

100g/4oz minced pork

1 onion, chopped

40g/1½oz butter

salt and pepper

No Smörgåsbord is complete without meat balls. This dish is very versatile; it goes with everything and everywhere. There are as many recipes as there are cooks.

Soak the breadcrumbs in the cream and water mixture. Mix together the minced beef, veal and pork. Fry the onion in a little of the butter until golden brown. Mix together the mince, onion, egg and soaked breadcrumbs. Work the mince until it is smooth. Season with salt and pepper.

Shape into balls and fry a few at a time in the remaining butter. Meat balls can be served with meat or chicken, in a soup or on their own hot or cold.

SWEETBREADS WITH GARLIC MAYONNAISE
KALVEBRISSEL MED HVITLØKMAJONES

SERVES 4

300g/10oz sweetbreads

boiled rice or lettuce leaves,
 to serve

STOCK

500ml/18fl oz water

½ tsp salt

5 peppercorns

sprig of parsley

1 carrot, sliced

½ onion, sliced

1 bay leaf

GARLIC MAYONNAISE

150ml/¼pt mayonnaise

50ml/2fl oz soured cream

1 clove garlic, crushed

2 tbsp chopped fresh parsley,
 dill and chives

The delicate taste of sweetbreads is enhanced by the garlic mayonnaise.

Place the sweetbreads in cold water and bring to the boil. Drain, then remove any dark parts and outer membranes. Bring all the stock ingredients to the boil and simmer for about 10 minutes. Place the sweetbreads in the stock and simmer for a further 10 minutes. Leave to cool in the stock.

Mix the mayonnaise and soured cream, garlic, parsley, dill and chives together. Cut the sweetbreads in slices. Place them on a bed of boiled rice or lettuce leaves. Pour a little mayonnaise on each slice. Serve with toasted bread and butter.

GOURMET LAMB

VORSCHMACK

SERVES 4–6

1 soaked salt herring or 2 Matjes
  herring fillets

8 anchovy fillets

1kg/2lb roast lamb

2 medium onions

½ tbsp butter for cooking

juice from the roast lamb or
  consommé

1 tbsp tomato sauce or purée

white pepper

2 tbsp mustard

90–100ml/3½–4fl oz single cream

Originating from Poland, Vorschmack was a favourite of Finland's national hero Field Marshall Mannerheim. It is very tasty as an appertizer or a late evening snack.

Clean and fillet the herring. Mince the fillets, anchovies, roast lamb and onions in a mincer or food processor.

Melt the butter in a saucepan, add the meat mixture and bring to the boil. Add a little meat juice or consommé until the mixture becomes porridge-like in consistency. Add the tomato sauce or purée and pepper to taste. Add the mustard and cream.

Simmer the lamb for 30 minutes, stirring occasionally to prevent sticking. Serve steaming hot with pickled cucumbers, pickled beetroots and soured cream. The traditional drink Ryyppy is served ice cold as an accompaniment to the meal.

RYYPPY

475ml/16fl oz aquavit

475ml/16fl oz vodka

200ml/7fl oz Noilly Prat vermouth

90ml/3½fl oz gin

This is a very traditional Finnish drink – and an extremely intoxicating one! It is served with Gourmet Lamb among other dishes.

Mix all the ingredients in a shaker and fill the glasses to the brim.

Fishermen returning to Oddenhaven in Denmark with their catch.

VENISON WITH GOAT'S CHEESE

DYRESTEG

SERVES 4–6

1.5kg/3lb venison joint

40g/1½oz softened butter

salt and ground black pepper

600ml/1pt beef stock

15g/½oz butter

1 tbsp plain flour

2 tsp redcurrant jelly

175g/6oz goat's cheese, diced

75ml/3fl oz soured cream

Reindeer meat is hard to find outside Scandinavia, venison is more readily available so this traditional dish has been made with venison. Prepared this way the meat will remain succulent. The sauce adds a special gourmet touch to this Norwegian speciality.

Preheat the oven to 240°C/475°F/Gas Mark 9. Tie the joint with string to keep its shape during cooking. Brush the meat with the softened butter. Place the meat on a rack in a roasting tin. Roast for 20 minutes. Lower the oven heat to 180°C/350°F/Gas Mark 4. Season generously with salt and a pinch of black pepper. Pour in the stock and roast for another hour, basting with the stock a few times.

Remove the meat and place in an ovenproof dish. Leave in the turned off oven with the door open. Skim the fat off the meat juice in the tin. Measure out 225ml/8fl oz meat juice, topping up with water if needed. Reheat.

Melt the 15g/½oz butter and stir in the flour. Cook for 2–3 minutes on a low heat, stirring continuously. Whisk in the meat juice, add the redcurrant jelly and diced goat's cheese. Keep whisking until the sauce is smooth. Add the soured cream and warm through, do not let the sauce boil. Season to taste. Slice the meat thinly and serve with the sauce.

Children during their Easter festivities in Finland.

SUMMER OMELETTE WITH SAUSAGES

SOMMERAEGGEHAGE MED POLSER

SERVES 4–6

6 tomatoes

½ cucumber

12 radishes

chives

5 frankfurters

15g/2½oz butter

8 eggs, size 4 or 5

100ml/4fl oz milk or single cream

pepper

It is the way in which this omelette is served that makes it typically Danish. Another example of a tasty dish, made with the easily obtainable canned Danish frankfurters.

Slice the tomatoes, cucumber and radishes, and chop the chives.

Slice the frankfurters and sauté in 15g/½oz of the butter. Beat the eggs a little and whisk in the milk or cream. Season with pepper. Heat the remaining butter in a non-stick frying pan and pour in the egg mixture. Add the sliced frankfurters, cook and stir constantly until set. Season to taste.

Serve the omelette on a serving dish surrounded by the tomatoes, cucumber and radishes. Sprinkle the chives on top.

PALACE STEAK
SLOTTSSTEK

SERVES 4–6

800g/1¾lb boneless beef (fillet
   or thick flank)
15g/½oz butter
1 tsp salt
6 whole allspice
6 white peppercorns
1 tsp pickling vinegar
1½ tbsp golden syrup
3–4 anchovy fillets
1 medium onion, chopped
1 bay leaf
300ml/½pt stock
50ml/2fl oz port

The traditional Swedish Palace Steak acquires its characteristic flavour from bay leaves, anchovies and a little pickling vinegar, similar to the Swedish beef stew.

Brown the steak on both sides in melted butter in a flameproof casserole. Sprinkle the salt on the meat and place the remaining spices, vinegar, syrup, anchovy fillets and onion and bay leaf in the casserole. Add some of the stock together with the port. Reduce the heat to low and cover. Simmer for 1½ hours. Add more stock during cooking and turn the meat occasionally. Test the meat is cooked through.

Sieve the gravy into a saucepan. Whisk the flour into a little water and add to thicken the gravy. Boil for a few minutes with the bay leaf and add the cream. Season to taste.

Slice the meat and cut into portions. Serve with boiled or sauté potatoes, fresh vegetables, the sauce and loganberry or black or redcurrant jelly.

SAUCE

400ml/14fl oz beef gravy	1 bay leaf
1½ tbsp plain flour	few peppercorns
50–100ml/2–4fl oz single cream	salt and pepper

◄ *Palace steak*

LAMB AND CABBAGE STEW
FÅR I KÅL

SERVES 4

1kg/2lb lamb on the bone, such
   as middle neck or breast
1kg/2lb white cabbage
25–40g/1–1½oz butter
1–2 tsp salt
10 white peppercorns
1 bay leaf
450ml/16fl oz water
chopped fresh parsley

Wholesome and warming, this stew uses economical cuts of lamb, is easy to prepare and has a real country flavour.

Trim the meat and cut into large cubes. Cut the cabbage into large pieces. Brown the meat and cabbage in the butter.

Alternate layers of meat and cabbage in a flameproof casserole dish. Sprinkle each layer with salt and pepper. Add the bay leaf and water. Cover the pan and bring to the boil. Skim off the fat, then simmer for 1½ hours or until tender. Sprinkle with chopped parsley and serve with boiled potatoes.

SWEDISH HASH

PYTT I PANNA

A useful way to deal with leftover meat. The smoked sausage or ham adds a distinctive flavour.

SERVES 4–6

25–40g/1–1½oz butter
2 medium onions, finely chopped
350g/12oz smoked sausage or
 ham, diced
8 boiled potatoes, diced
350g/12oz leftover meat, diced
salt and pepper
chopped fresh parsley

Melt half of the butter in a frying pan and gently fry the onions until golden brown. Remove to a platter and add the remaining butter to the pan. Fry the smoked sausage or ham together with the diced potatoes. Add the fried onions and diced leftover meat. Mix gently. Season to taste and heat thoroughly. Sprinkle the chopped parsley on top. Serve piping hot with raw egg yolk or fried egg, fresh cucumber salad or pickled beetroot.

Swedish hash ▶

MEAT PATTIES
FRIKADELLER

Frikadeller are as Danish as their flag, Danneborg, and there are as many variations as there are cooks. This dish can be eaten either hot or cold.

SERVES 4–6

50g/2oz butter

2 tbsp oil

1 medium onion, chopped

225g/8oz minced veal

225g/8oz minced pork

3 tbsp plain flour

350ml/12fl oz soda water

1 egg, size 4 or 5

1 tsp salt

pepper

Melt a little of the butter and oil and fry the onion until golden brown. Mix the minced veal and pork together in a bowl with the flour. Slowly stir in the soda water until light and fluffy. Add the onion to the mixture. Whisk in the egg, salt and pepper, cover the bowl and leave to cool for 1 hour.

Form the mince mixture into balls or hamburger shapes. Melt the remaining butter and oil and fry the patties for about 15 minutes. Serve with boiled potatoes, pickled beetroot or red cabbage.

EASTER CHICKEN CASSEROLE
PASKEKYLLING MED AEGGARNITURE

SERVES 4–6

50g/2oz butter
1.5kg/3lb chicken joints
3 medium onions, chopped
600ml/1pt chicken stock
225g/8oz mushrooms
2 tbsp chopped fresh parsley
salt and pepper
225g/8oz peas
2 eggs, size 4 or 5
2 tbsp milk
butter for cooking
2 tbsp cornflour

This dish is traditionally served on Easter Monday with decorated eggs, new potatoes, carrots and peas followed by a cheese board and a sweet.

Melt the butter and fry the chicken joints and onions until golden brown. Add the chicken stock, mushrooms and 1 tbsp of the chopped parsley and season with salt and pepper. Cover and simmer for 35 minutes, adding the peas for the last 5–8 minutes.

Beat the eggs and milk together and season. Fry the egg mixture in a little butter in an omelette pan until firm. Put the chicken and vegetables on a heated serving dish and keep warm. Thicken the cooking liquid with the cornflour blended with water to make the gravy. Pour the gravy over the chicken and vegetables. Cut the fried egg into thin strips and use to garnish the chicken with the remaining chopped parsley.

Easter chicken casserole ▶

LIVER AND RICE CASSEROLE
MAKSALAATIKKO

SERVES 6–8

40g/14oz white long grain rice
3.25 litres/6pt boiling salted water
40g/1½oz butter
1 medium onion, finely chopped
450ml/¾pt milk
2 eggs, lightly beaten
4 slices of streaky bacon, cooked
  and diced
100g/4oz raisins
2 tbsp golden syrup
2 tsp salt
1 tsp white pepper
1 tsp ground marjoram
700g/1½lb calf's or ox liver, minced

The baking oven came from the east more than a thousand years ago. The old, tried and true Finnish dishes still depend on the oven. In fact, most Finnish cooking makes heavy use of the oven.

Cook the rice in the boiling salted water for about 12 minutes, then drain and put aside. Melt 25g/1oz butter in a frying pan and gently sauté the onion until golden. Remove and put aside.

Preheat the oven to 170°C/325°F/Gas Mark 3. In a large bowl, carefully combine the cooked rice, the milk and beaten eggs. Add the onion, diced bacon, raisins and golden syrup. Season with salt, pepper and marjoram. Stir in the minced liver and mix thoroughly.

Grease an ovenproof dish and add the liver and rice mixture. Bake, uncovered, for 1–1½ hours. Serve with green salad and loganberry or cranberry sauce.

ROAST GOOSE
GAASE STEG

SERVES 8–10

225g/8oz prunes, stoned

4–4.5kg/9–10lb goose

juice of 1 lemon

225g/8oz apples, cored and
  peeled

1 tbsp salt

600ml/1pt chicken stock or water

1 tbsp sugar

pepper

The main dish at the Christmas table is roast goose. Danish tradition demands the goose be stuffed with peeled and sliced apples and prunes. It is served with cooked apples stuffed with prunes and the recipe for this is on page 86.

Soak the prunes in water for 12 hours. Preheat the oven to 180°C/350°F/Gas Mark 4. Rinse the goose thoroughly under cold running water. Dry with absorbent kitchen paper. Brush the goose both inside and out with the juice from the lemon and then rub the inside of the goose with the sugar, pepper and onion. Cut the prunes and apples into small pieces, sprinkle with salt and place inside the goose. Secure with skewers or sew the skin together. Sprinkle with salt. Place the goose in a baking tin and put it on the bottom oven shelf. Roast for about 20 minutes to brown.

Drain off the fat and pour the boiling stock or water, sugar and pepper into the tin. Turn the goose over so the back is facing up and roast for 1 hour. Turn it breast up and roast for a further 1½–2 hours. Leave for 15 minutes in the switched off oven with the door open. Remove the stuffing and discard it – it is too fatty to eat.

Serve the goose with apples stuffed with prunes (page 86), red cabbage (page 82) and caramelized potatoes (page 94).

*A traditional thatched-roof barn in
Skansen, Stockholm.*

GROUSE WITH CREAM SAUCE

RIEKKO KERMAKASTIKKEESSA

SERVES 4–6

15–25g/½–1oz butter

2 grouse, cleaned

2 tsp salt

¼ tsp pepper

400–425ml/14–15fl oz
consommé

SAUCE

about 250ml/9fl oz juice from
the birds

2–3 tbsp plain flour

225m/8fl oz cream

salt

Finns love the taste of game – some even prepare chicken to taste like game. They rub it inside and out with a mixture of chopped pine needles and juniper berries. The chicken is then left to hang for a few days before roasting it to get the flavour of game.

Melt the butter in a frying pan and fry the birds. Sprinkle with salt and pepper. Add the consommé and bring to the boil. Reduce the heat and simmer for about 45 minutes until tender. Keep the birds warm.

Strain the juice from the frying pan into a saucepan and whisk in the flour and heat gently. Add the juice from the birds, whisking all the time. Stir in the cream and season to taste. Simmer for a few minutes.

Remove the meat from the bones and place in a heated serving dish. Pour the cream sauce over the birds. Serve with boiled potatoes, vegetables, mushrooms, berries or redcurrant jelly.

EASTER VEAL

PASKEKALV

SERVES 4–6

1kg/2lb boneless leg of veal

1.1 litres/2pt veal or chicken
stock

5 carrots, sliced

15 shallots or very small onions

Bouquet garni of 5 sprigs of
parsley, 1 stick of sliced celery,
1 bay leaf, 4 white peppercorns
and ¼ tsp thyme, tied in muslin

1½ tsp salt

50g/2oz butter

25g/1oz plain flour

2 egg yolks, beaten

1½ tbsp lemon juice

225g/8oz mushrooms, sautéed

This is another traditional dish, very often served during Easter celebrations.

Boil the meat for 5 minutes in water, ensuring the meat is covered. Remove the froth and drain. Put the meat into a deep saucepan and add the stock, carrots, shallots and the bouquet garni. Add a little salt. Bring to the boil, skimming off any froth. Simmer for 1–11/2 hours until tender.

Remove the meat, carrots and shallots. Strain the liquid. Melt the butter, add the flour and cook for 2–3 minutes, stirring continuously. Gradually add the stock, stirring until the mixture is thick and smooth. Remove from the heat. Add the beaten egg yolks with the lemon juice. Stir in the sautéed mushrooms. Slice the meat and serve with rice or mashed potatoes.

CREAMED SWEETBREADS

KALVBRÄSS

SERVES 4–6

450g/1lb sweetbreads

25–50g/1–2oz butter

1 medium carrot, sliced

1 small onion

1 bay leaf

¼ tsp dried thyme

sprig of parsley

4–5 white peppercorns

500ml/18fl oz chicken stock or
   water

butter for cooking

1–2 tbsp plain flour

300ml/½pt double or whipping
   cream

salt and pepper

sherry (optional)

Delicious served on its own or on toast. But superlative as a filling for omelettes or vol au vents. The preparation is simple and the result is delicious – well worth the time spent.

Clean the sweetbreads, removing any blood vessels and membranes. Soak in cold water for about 1 hour. Bring to the boil in lightly salted water. Rinse under cold running water.

Put a knob of butter, the carrot, onion, bay leaf, thyme, parsley and peppercorns into a saucepan. Place the sweetbreads on top and leave to sweat over a low heat for 5 minutes. Cover the sweetbreads with chicken stock or water and add salt to taste. Place a lid on the saucepan and boil for 10 minutes.

Put the sweetbreads in a bowl and strain the liquid over. Leave to cool. Cut the sweetbreads into small pieces and fry lightly in the remaining butter. Sprinkle with the flour and continue to fry lightly for a few minutes. Add the cream, stirring continuously until thick and smooth. Season with salt and pepper; you may add a little sherry if you wish for taste.

Café society in the streets of Copenhagen.

FILLET OF VEAL A LA OSCAR

KALVFILE OSCAR

SERVES 4–6

6 slices of veal fillet or thick flank
  (600–700g/1¼–1½lb)

salt and white pepper

2 tbsp plain flour for coating

30g/1oz butter

1 small can asparagus tips

1 small cooked lobster or 1 can
  of crab

CHORON SAUCE

2 tbsp vinegar

15ml/1 tbsp water

6 crushed white peppercorns

1 tbsp finely chopped onion

a few parsley stalks

½ tsp dried tarragon

½ tsp dried chervil

3 egg yolks

200g/7oz butter or margarine

2 tbsp tomato purée

This dish, with its royal connotations, as the name suggests, should be made from fillet of veal with lobster and asparagus to garnish. But as veal fillet is expensive, thick flank can be used instead, with apologies to King Oscar.

For the sauce, mix the vinegar, water, peppercorns, onion and herbs in a heavy saucepan. Bring to the boil and reduce by half. Strain and pour back into the pan. Stand the pan in a simmering bain marie and add the yolks, whisking hard. Continue whisking until the mixture is thick and fluffy. Melt the butter or margarine, then pour into the mixture slowly, whisking vigorously. Add the tomato purée, a little at a time. Leave the sauce in the bain marie while the meat is being prepared.

Flatten the meat slices, season with salt and pepper, then coat in the flour. Fry in a pan in half the butter for 4 minutes on each side. Place on a warm serving dish.

Warm the asparagus in the remaining butter. Place a couple of asparagus tips, with a few pieces of lobster meat or crab and one or two tablespoons of Choron Sauce with each slice of meat. Serve with sauté potatoes and salad.

PIGS' TROTTERS

SIANSORKKA

SERVES 4–6

1.75–2.25kg/4–5lb pigs'
  trotters, preferably forelegs

3.25 litres/6pt water

4 tsp salt

20 whole white peppercorns

2–3 bay leaves

Lent is traditionally a time for outdoor get-togethers, where lanterns and candles are placed in trees. It requires food that can be prepared beforehand.

Rinse the trotters well in cold water. Place in a saucepan, cover with the cold water and bring to the boil. Skim off any foam and season with the salt, peppercorns and bay leaves. Simmer over low heat for 2–3 hours until tender. Leave to cool in the pan. Remove and serve cold. This dish is easiest eaten with your fingers.

5

VEGETABLE DISHES AND SALADS

FRESH MUSHROOM SALAD
SIENISALAATTI

SERVES 4–6

175ml/6fl oz water

1 tbsp lemon juice

225g/8oz fresh mushrooms,
  sliced

50ml/2fl oz double cream

1 tbsp grated onion

pinch of sugar

2 tsp salt

½ tsp white pepper

lettuce leaves

As with wild berries, picking mushrooms is universally enjoyed. Each mushroom has its own shape, taste and character. There are hundreds of edible varieties. Mushrooms can be used in salads, soups and sauces.

Bring the water and lemon juice to the boil. Add the mushrooms and cover. Reduce the heat and simmer for 2–3 minutes. Drain the mushrooms and dry on absorbent kitchen paper.

In a bowl, mix the cream, onion, sugar, salt and pepper, toss the mushrooms in the mixture. Serve on crisp dry lettuce leaves.

Fresh mushroom salad ▶

JANSSON'S TEMPTATION
JANSSONS FRESTELSE

SERVES 4–6

6 medium potatoes

10 anchovies in brine

2 medium onions, thinly sliced

25–50g/1–2oz butter

250ml/9fl oz double cream

No wonder Jansson was tempted! The saltiness of the anchovies is tempered by the potatoes. Onions add a contrasting flavour and the cream makes this dish irresistible.

Preheat the oven to 170°C/325°F/Gas Mark 3. Peel the potatoes and cut into thin strips. Soak them in cold water to get rid of the starch – it will make the potatoes crispier. Meanwhile, cut the anchovy fillets in half, if preferred. Reserve the brine. Fry the onions gently in half the butter until golden brown.

Grease an ovenproof dish. Dry the potatoes with absorbent kitchen paper. Put the potatoes, anchovies and onions in layers, beginning and finishing with potato. Pour over half of the cream. Dot with the remaining butter and 4 tbsp anchovy brine. Bake for about 25 minutes. Pour over the rest of the cream and anchovy brine. Bake for another 20 minutes. Serve with cold beer.

RED CABBAGE

RØDKAAL

SERVES 4–6

1.5kg/3lb red cabbage

40g/1½oz butter

1–2 tbsp sugar

50ml/2fl oz water

50ml/2fl oz malt vinegar

salt and pepper

2 medium tart apples

150g/5oz redcurrant jelly

This piquant colourful dish complements most dishes very well. Red cabbage tastes better if made the day before, then reheated. Equally delicious served cold – popular in Denmark on Boxing Day.

Shred the cabbage. Melt the butter in a large frying pan and stir in the sugar. Add the cabbage and cook for 5 minutes, stirring continuously. Add the water, vinegar, salt and pepper. Cover and simmer for 2–3 hours until tender. Peel and grate the apples and add to the cabbage with the redcurrant jelly.

The lake at Oldevatre – Norway's beautiful wilderness at its best.

HOT POTATO SALAD WITH BACON
VARM POTETSALAT MED BACON

SERVES 4

100g/4oz bacon rashers

8–10 boiled cold potatoes, sliced

1 medium onion, finely chopped

about 25g/1oz chopped fresh
  parsley

1–1½ tbsp wine vinegar

1–2 tbsp water

salt and pepper

Hot potato salad, flavoured with bacon pieces and sharpened with hint of wine vinegar, is a tasty way to serve potatoes. It is quick and easy to prepare and very good to serve with sausages or other meat.

Cut the bacon rashers into strips and fry until crisp. Place the potatoes and other ingredients in the frying pan. Stir carefully to mix. Place the lid on the pan and heat the salad carefully for 5–6 minutes. The potatoes must not brown. Serve with meat and sausages.

CHICORY AU GRATIN
GRATINERAD ENDIVE

SERVES 2

about 4 chicory spears, sliced

100g/4oz ham, cubed

50g/2oz butter

2 tbsp plain flour

300ml/½pt hot milk

salt and pepper

1 tbsp tomato purée or red wine

grated cheese for topping

A very tasty gratin using ham, or bacon if liked. Alternatively, use smoked fish or prawns to give it a totally different, but nonetheless, delicious character. If prawns are used, substitute 100ml/4fl oz white wine for 100ml/4fl oz of the milk.

Place a layer of sliced chicory in an ovenproof dish. Sprinkle with fried cubes of ham.

Melt half the butter, add the flour and cook for 2–3 minutes, stirring. Gradually stir in the hot milk. Season the sauce with salt and pepper, a little tomato purée or red wine. Pour over the chicory. Sprinkle plenty of grated cheese on top and dot with the remaining butter. Bake for about 20 minutes until the chicory is cooked and the topping is golden.

SWEDE CASSEROLE
LANTTULAATIKKO

SERVES 4–6

2 medium swedes or 1kg/2lb
  turnips, peeled

1½ tsp salt

4 tsp breadcrumbs

50ml/2fl oz double cream

½ tsp grated nutmeg

2 eggs, size 4 or 5, lightly beaten

25g/1oz butter

This casserole is a glorified bubble and squeak. In fact, any vegetables can be used. If made with carrots only it is called Porkhanalaatikko.

Dice the swedes into 8mm/¼in pieces and put into a saucepan. Cover with cold water, add ½ tsp of the salt and bring to the boil. Lower the heat and simmer for about 20 minutes until soft. Drain the swedes and purée in a blender.

Preheat the oven to 170°C/325°F/Gas Mark 3. Soak the breadcrumbs in the cream for a few minutes. Stir in the nutmeg, remaining salt and beaten eggs. Add the puréed swede and mix thoroughly.

Grease a 2.25litre/4pt casserole dish and pour in the mixture. Cut the butter into tiny pieces and dot over the swedes. Bake, uncovered, for about 1 hour until golden brown. Serve with meat or fish, or on its own.

LACY POTATO PANCAKES WITH CHIVES
RÅRAKOR

SERVES 4–6

4 medium potatoes

2 tbsp chopped fresh chives

2 tbsp salt

freshly ground black pepper

25g/1oz butter

2 tbsp vegetable oil

Chives add the flavour of spring to this dish and the crispy lacy texture provided by the grated potatoes makes these pancakes delightfully different.

Peel the potatoes and grate them coarsely into a large bowl. Do not drain off the potato water which accumulates in the bowl. Working quickly to prevent the potatoes from turning brown, add the chopped chives, salt and a little pepper.

Heat the butter and oil in a 25cm/10in frying pan. When very hot, add 2 tbsp potato mixture for each pancake. Fry on both sides for 2–3 minutes until golden brown. Flatten them with a spatula during cooking. Serve straight away.

COOKED APPLES STUFFED WITH PRUNES
KOGT AEBLER MED SVEDSKER

SERVES 4–8

225g/8oz sugar

port to taste

16 prunes

8 large apples, cored and peeled

900ml/1½pt cold water

Serve these port-flavoured prune and apple halves hot with goose or duck.

Put 2 tsp sugar, the port and prunes in an ovenproof dish. Leave to macerate for 6–8 hours. Preheat the oven to 170°C/325°F/Gas Mark 3. Cook for 20–30 minutes until soft.

Cut the apples in half. Mix the remaining sugar and water in a pan then boil for 2–3 minutes. Add the apples and leave to simmer for 10 minutes, uncovered, over a low heat. Remove the apples with a slotted spoon and place in a serving dish. Put one prune on each apple half

POTATO CAKE WITH ROSEMARY
POTETKAKE MED ROSMARIN

SERVES 4–6

8 potatoes

50g/2oz margarine or butter

1 tsp fresh or ½ tsp dried rosemary

1½ tsp salt

A simple but delicious way to serve potatoes. Pressing the potatoes together whilst cooking forms a crisp "cake".

Peel the potatoes and slice thinly. Rinse and dry them well. Melt the margarine or butter in a frying pan and brown the potato slices carefully. Sprinkle with the rosemary and salt.

Press the potato slices well together and fry them over a low heat until they are tender and the cake has a nice colour underneath. Turn the cake over and fry until lightly browned. Serve with meat and fish dishes.

BUTTON MUSHROOM
AND BROCCOLI GRATIN
KANTARELLGRATINERT BROCCOLI

SERVES 4–6

450g/1lb fresh broccoli

salt

SAUCE

200g/7oz button mushrooms

15g/½oz butter

1½ tbsp plain flour

300ml/½pt cream

½–1 tsp salt

1 tbsp grated cheese

A gratin of broccoli with button mushrooms – a simple dish retaining the full flavour of the vegetables.

Boil the broccoli in salted water until tender. Drain and place in a buttered ovenproof dish. Cut the mushrooms into small pieces and fry them quickly in the butter. Drain any liquid into a separate container. Sprinkle the mushrooms with the flour, stirring. Add the cream and reserved liquid and boil for a couple of minutes, stirring. Pour over the broccoli and sprinkle with the cheese. Brown for 5–8 minutes. Serve with meat or fish, or on its own.

STUFFED ONIONS
LÖKDOLMAR

SERVES 4–6

3–4 large yellow onions

1 tbsp breadcrumbs

100ml/4fl oz single cream

150g/5oz minced veal or
  cooked rice

1 small can of mushrooms

1 egg yolk

salt and white pepper

celery salt

25g/1oz butter

Old fashioned, lovely stuffed onions are a delicacy, well worth a revival in their popularity. It is difficult to understand why this fine dish has been forgotten.

Peel the onions and make a deep cut through half of each onion. Boil the onions until semi-soft in lightly salted water. Drain, reserving the cooking liquid, then rinse them under cold water. Separate the layers carefully and leave to drain. Take the cores of the onions and chop finely.

Stir the breadcrumbs into the cream and leave to swell. Mix with the mince or rice, mushrooms, chopped onion cores and egg yolk. Season well with salt, pepper and celery salt.

Place 1 tbsp of the mixture on every large onion layer and fold. Melt the butter in a frying pan and brown the stuffed onion layers all over. Add 150ml/¼pt of the onion water and simmer, covered, until soft. Add more onion water if needed.

Stuffed onions can also be baked in a greased ovenproof dish. First brush with melted butter or margarine, then bake in the oven at 220°C/425°F/Gas Mark 7 for 30 minutes.

Stuffed onions ▶

VEGETABLE SALAD
ROSOLLI

Rosolli is very often eaten as a great savoury pick-me-up on Christmas Eve morning.

SERVES 6

7 fresh beetroots

5 potatoes

7 carrots

2 apples

2 medium onions

3 large sprigs fresh dill or
   1½ tsp dill seed

salt

Boil the beetroot and potatoes in their skins with the carrots until tender. Refrigerate for 2–3 hours. Peel and chop the cooked vegetables, apples and onions and chop the dill. Mix them all together and season with salt, tossing a few times. Serve with salad cream.

Vegetable salad ▶

COLESLAW
VITKÅLS SALAD

So easy to prepare, the taste of this coleslaw is much more individual than supermarket versions. It is a healthy accompaniment to cold meats.

SERVES 4–6

1 small cabbage

1 small leek

5–6 carrots

6 pickled gherkins

DRESSING

100 ml/4fl oz oil

100 ml/4fl oz cider vinegar

25g/1oz sugar (or less sugar with a spoonful of honey)

1 tsp salt

1½ tsp coarsely ground black pepper

a little lemon juice

Finely shred the cabbage and leek. Coarsely grate the carrots and chop the gherkins.

Bring the dressing ingredients to the boil in a saucepan. Pour the hot dressing over the vegetables. Serve cold.

WEST COAST SALAD
VÄSTKUSTSALLAD

SERVES 4–6

200g/7oz cooked fresh prawns

1 cooked fresh lobster or crab or
 175g/6oz canned

2 tomatoes

100g/4oz mushrooms, sliced

1 lettuce, shredded

1 small can asparagus and/or
 1 small packet frozen peas

125g/4½ oz packet frozen
 sweetcorn

3 pickled gherkins

hard-boiled egg wedges, to
 garnish

◄ *West Coast salad*

Serve this salad for lunch or supper, or as a starter. This light and delicious salad can be prepared in advance and kept in the refrigerator. Add the dressing just before serving.

Peel the prawns. Pick the meat from the lobster or crab and cut into small pieces. Cut the tomatoes into thin wedges. Mix and gently stir the seafood, mushrooms, lettuce and tomatoes together. Blend with the asparagus and/or peas, sweetcorn and gherkins. Chill before serving. Shake the dressing ingredients together and pour over the salad. Garnish with hard-boiled eggs, cut in wedges.

DRESSING

2 tbsp red wine vinegar

salt and white pepper

6 tbsp oil

KALE IN CREAM SAUCE
GRØNKÅL MØD FLØDE

SERVES 4–6

450g/1lb kale

2 tsp salt

50g/2oz butter

4 tbsp plain flour

225ml/8fl oz milk

225ml/8fl oz whipping or
 double cream

½ tsp freshly ground pepper

Vegetables which keep well through the winter play a large part in Danish cooking. Kale served this way makes an excellent side dish to accompany cured loin of pork, a favourite traditional dish.

Pick the tender kale leaves from the stalks and wash thoroughly under cold running water. Shake off the water and tear the leaves into large pieces. Cook the kale in boiling salted water for about 10–15 minutes. Drain thoroughly, then finely chop the kale.

For the sauce, melt the butter in a pan. Remove from the heat and stir in the flour. Pour in the milk and cream at the same time, whisking vigorously. Return the pan to a low heat, whisking continuously, until smooth. Season to taste. Add the finely chopped kale and heat for a few minutes.

CARAMELIZED POTATOES
BRUNEDE KARTOFLER

SERVES 4–6

700g/1½lb small potatoes

25g/1oz sugar

25g/1oz butter

The potato came to Denmark around 1760. These sweet tasting potatoes were served as a treat in the olden days. Now they are part of the Danish Christmas table.

Boil the potatoes in their skins. Melt the sugar in a deep frying pan. When golden, add the butter. Peel the potatoes. Toss gently in the sugar and butter mixture until warm and well glazed.

6

DESSERTS

SOURED CREAM WAFFLES

FLOTEVAFLER

In the past, many families owned special irons made and embossed by the local blacksmiths with individual patterns. However, these waffles are just as delicious made with a modern waffle iron.

SERVES 6

5 eggs, size 4 or 5
100g/4oz sugar
100g/4oz plain flour
1 tsp ground cardamom or ginger
175ml/6fl oz soured cream
50g/2oz butter

Mix the eggs and sugar for about 5 minutes until fluffy. Whisk in the flour, cardamom or ginger and soured cream. Whisk until smooth and creamy. Melt the butter and stir it into the mixture. Set aside for 10 minutes. Cook in a waffle iron according to the manufacturer's instructions. Serve with jam, cream or sugar.

Soured cream waffles ▶

EASTER DESSERT

PASKEDESSERT

Rich and delicious, "chocoholics" won't be able to keep away from this Norwegian speciality.

SERVES 4–6

100g/4oz butter
100g/4oz chocolate
6 eggs, separated
100g/4oz sugar
100g/4oz ground almonds
cream, to decorate

Preheat the oven to 180°C/350°F/Gas Mark 4. Melt the butter and chocolate together in a pan, stirring the mixture until it foams. Well whisk the egg yolks and sugar, then add to the chocolate mixture. Whisk the egg whites. Stir the ground almonds and finally the whisked egg whites into the mixture.

Grease a 23cm/9in baking tin and sprinkle with flour. Place the mixture in the tin and stand the tin in a baking dish half filled with water. Bake for about 45 minutes. Serve cold and decorate with cream.

HONEYED PEACHES
HONUNGSPERSIKOR

Just sit back and wait for the compliments when you serve this delectable yet simple-to-prepare dessert.

SERVES 4–6

4 large fresh peaches or 1 large
  can peach halves
4 tbsp honey
juice of 2 oranges
2–3 tbsp water
juice of 1 lemon, if using canned
  peaches

FILLING

4 tbsp ground almonds
4 tbsp sugar
50 g/2oz butter, softened

Scald, peel, halve and remove the stone from the fresh peaches. Leave canned peaches to drain. Melt the honey in a shallow pan. Add the orange juice and water. Add the lemon juice, if necessary. Bring the syrup to the boil and add the peach halves. Simmer until soft, turning them now and then.

Preheat the oven to 200°C/400°F/Gas Mark 6. Place the peach halves, rounded side down, in an ovenproof dish and pour the syrup over. Mix together the ground almonds, sugar and softened butter. Divide the filling between the peaches. Bake the peaches until the filling is golden. Leave to cool slightly, then serve with vanilla ice cream.

BLUEBERRY PIE
MUSTIKKAPIIRAKKA

SERVES 4–6

CRUST

175g/6oz butter

75g/3oz sugar (optional)

1 egg, size 4 or 5

75ml/3fl oz whipping cream

250g/9oz plain flour

FILLING

900ml/1½pt blueberries

sugar to taste (optional)

1 tsp breadcrumbs or potato flour

Berries are loved by the Finns and there are plenty for picking in the forests.

Soften the butter and add the sugar, if using. Mix in the egg thoroughly, then add the cream and flour. Mix well but do not beat the dough. Leave the dough to stand in a cool place for 15 minutes.

Preheat the oven to 200°C/400°F/Gas Mark 6. Roll out the dough into a thin sheet and transfer to a greased baking sheet, shaping a raised edge all the way round. Mix the blueberries with the sugar, if using, and the breadcrumbs or potato flour. Spread the filling on the dough. Bake until the crust is golden brown.

Blueberry pie ▶

FRUIT SALAD WITH EGG SAUCE
HIMMELSK LAPSKAUS EGGDOSIS

SERVES 4–6

200g/7oz ripe bananas, diced
   or sliced

200g/7oz seedless grapes,
   halved

175g/6oz crisp apples or
   oranges, diced

175g/6oz hazelnuts or walnuts,
   chopped

juice of 1 lemon

EGG SAUCE

5 egg yolks

2 egg whites

5 tbsp sugar

1 tbsp cognac or rum

A refreshing fruit salad served with a creamy smooth sauce, flavoured with cognac or rum.

Mix the fruit and nuts together in a bowl. Add the lemon juice to prevent the fruit from browning. Refrigerate for 20 minutes. Chill a serving dish for the sauce.

For the sauce, mix the egg yolks, egg whites and sugar in a food processor at medium speed. When the mixture thickens, add the cognac or rum. Serve immediately in a chilled serving dish together with the fruit.

RASPBERRY TART

BRINGEBÆR KAKE

SERVES 6

PASTRY

225g/8oz plain flour
pinch of salt
100g/4oz soft butter
25g/1oz sugar
1 egg yolk

LEMON CREAM

2 egg yolks
2 tbsp sugar
¾ tbsp cornflour
250ml/9fl oz single cream
2 tbsp softened butter
grated rind of ¼–½ lemon

DECORATION

gelatine
200ml/7fl oz water
2 tbsp sugar
juice of ½ lemon
about 300g/10oz fresh
  raspberries or 225g/8oz
  packet of frozen raspberries

Delicious fresh tart consisting of a thin rich shortcrust shell filled with a fine lemon cream and raspberries, topped with lemon jelly. Suitable both for tea and as a dessert.

Preheat the oven to 180°C/200°F/Gas Mark 5. Place the flour and salt in a bowl, then rub in the butter until the mixture resembles breadcrumbs. Stir in the sugar. Add the egg yolk and stir until it forms a dough. Add water as necessary. Knead lightly. Use to line a flan tin, about 23cm/9in in diameter. Bake blind for about 10 minutes until golden. Cool slightly, then release carefully from the tin.

For the lemon cream, whisk together the egg yolks, cream, cornflour and sugar in a saucepan. Simmer the mixture, whisking, until the cream is thick and fluffy. Remove from the heat, add the butter and whisk occasionally while it cools. Flavour the cold cream with the lemon rind.

Dissolve the gelatine in the water for the jelly. Add the sugar, lemon juice and squeezed gelatine leaves.

Fill the pastry shell with the lemon cream and cover with raspberries. Pour the jelly over when it starts to set. Leave the tart in a cold place until serving.

Raspberry tart ▶

TROLL'S DESSERT

TROLLKREM

SERVES 4

2 egg whites
200ml/⅓pt lightly sweetened
  apple sauce or
  225g/8oz fresh or frozen
  strawberries, sliced

Whip up this light troll dessert flavoured with fruit sauce or sliced strawberries and you will have a delightful dessert in no time.

Whisk the egg whites until stiff. Add the apple sauce or strawberries. Continue whisking until the mixture is stiff and fruit and egg whites are well blended. Use an electric whisk for quick results. Serve with cream.

LEMON SOUFFLE

CITRONFROMAGE

A most light and refreshing dessert for the palate, especially after a strong flavoured main course. To serve attractively, place the soufflé in tall glasses topped with piped whipped cream and decorated with glacé cherries.

SERVES 4

powdered gelatine
grated rind and juice of 1 lemon
4 eggs, size 4 or 5, separated
75g/3oz sugar
150ml/¼pt whipping cream

Soak the gelatine in the lemon juice. Whisk the egg whites until stiff. Dissolve the gelatine mixture in a bowl over a saucepan of hot water. Remove from the heat and stir in the egg yolks and grated lemon rind. Fold the sugar into the egg whites and fold gently into the lemon mixture. Pour the mixture into a glass dish and leave to set in the refrigerator. Serve with whipped cream.

APPLES WITH MERINGUE

EPLER MED MARENGS

Set in a "sea" of custard cream, topped with meringue, this attractive dessert gives apples a new look.

SERVES 4–6

5–6 apples
100g/4oz sugar
25g/1oz plain flour
1–2 eggs
250ml/9fl oz cold milk
1 tsp vanilla essence

MERINGUE

4 egg whites
125g/4½oz caster sugar

Preheat the oven to 180°C/350°F/Gas Mark 4. Peel and core the apples. Bake for about 50 minutes until tender. Whisk the sugar, flour and eggs in a pan. Add the milk and vanilla essence and cook until it thickens, stirring all the time.

   Pour the custard cream into a shallow ovenproof dish and place the baked apples on top. For the meringue, whip the egg whites until stiff. Fold in the sugar. Cover the apples with the meringue. Sprinkle with sugar and decorate with fruit, if liked. Bake for about 30 minutes until the meringue has set.

Apples with meringue ▶

RUM PUDDING

ROMPUDDING

Eggs given a royal treatment with a touch of rum and whipped cream. The careful preparation is well rewarded.

SERVES 4–6

300ml/½pt milk

2 eggs, separated

75g/3oz sugar

gelatine

50ml/2fl oz hot water

50ml/2fl oz rum

300ml/½pt whipping cream

Bring the milk to the boil. Whisk the egg yolks and sugar in a bowl for 15 minutes. Whisk in the milk, a little at a time. Return the mixture to the saucepan and stir constantly until it thickens. Pour into a bowl for cooling.

Dissolve the gelatine in the hot water. Whisk the egg whites until stiff. Add the dissolved gelatine, rum and whisked egg whites to the cooled mixture. Pour into a 900ml/½pt sugared and dampened mould. Leave to set for 30 minutes in the refrigerator. Turn out and serve decorated with whipped cream.

EASTER CHEESE CAKE

PASHA

SERVES 4–6

1.25/2½lb curd cheese

200g/7oz butter

1 egg, size 4 or 5

3 egg yolks, size 4 or 5

150g/5oz sugar

200ml/7fl oz whipping cream

1 split vanilla pod

50g/2oz candied orange peel

50g/2oz candied lemon peel

50g/2oz ground almonds

50g/2oz sultanas

½ tbsp ground cloves

½ tbsp ground cinnamon

2 tbsp lemon juice

20 whole almonds

glacé cherries

Karelia is perhaps the greatest single influence on the Finnish kitchen. For centuries Karelia was the point of entry for many dishes out of the east. Some bear the unmistakable stamp of Russia. The most traditional Easter sweet is the Russian Pasha, a cheese cake.

Put the cheese into a piece of muslin and squeeze out the liquid. Melt the butter and mix with the cheese. Cream the whole egg and egg yolks with the sugar. Gradually whisk in the cream and add the vanilla pod. Put the bowl over a pan of simmering water over a low heat. Stir the mixture until it becomes thick and creamy. Remove from the heat and continue stirring until cooled. Remove the vanilla pod, then fold in the curd cheese. Stir in the candied peels, ground almonds, sultanas, cloves, cinnamon and lemon juice.

Line a 1.2 litre/2 pt earthenware mould with a large dampened piece of muslin and spoon in the mixture. Fold the muslin loosely over the top and place a weight on top. Leave to stand for 1–2 days. Turn out the Pasha onto a serving dish. Decorate with almonds and glacé cherries.

Easter cheese cake ▶

CRANBERRY PARFAIT

KARPALOJAADYKE

SERVES 4–6

2 egg yolks, size 4 or 5

150g/5oz sugar

150ml/¼pt cranberry purée

400ml/14fl oz double cream

A parfait is a stylish and always successful dessert. Any berries can be used.

Whisk the egg yolks and sugar until fluffy. Stir in the cranberry purée. Whip the cream and fold gently into the cranberry mixture. Taste to see if more sugar is needed.

Rinse a 600–900ml/1–1½pt mould with cold water. Pour in the mixture and freeze. To remove parfait before serving, dip the mould into hot water for a few seconds. Serve with fresh berries and whipped cream.

PRUNE FOOL

LUUMUKIISSELI

SERVES 4–6

450g/1lb dried prunes, stoned

1.4 litres/2½pt water

100g/4oz sugar

1 stick of cinnamon

5 tbsp cornflour

TOPPING

2 tbsp sugar

300ml/½pt double or
  whipping cream

This traditional dessert is from western Finland.

Soak the prunes in cold water overnight. The next day, put the prunes and the soaking liquid in a saucepan and add the sugar and cinnamon stick. Cook until the prunes are soft. Remove the cinnamon stick.

Thicken the prune mixture with the cornflour mixed with a little cold water. Pour into dessert bowls and sprinkle the 2 tbsp sugar on top. Cool to room temperature. Serve with whipped cream on top or separately.

RHUBARB PUDDING
RABARBER COMPOTE

SERVES 4–6

1kg/2lb rhubarb

450g/1lb sugar

2–3 tbsp cornflour

50ml/2fl oz water

1 tsp vanilla essence

This pudding is also called "Constitution Day Pudding" with its red and white colours representing the national flag. On 5th June 1849, the king transferred the power to the people and it is a half day public holiday. Rhubarb can be cooked in lemonade instead of sugar and water.

Cut the rhubarb into pieces and put into a saucepan. Spoon over most of the sugar and add enough water to cover. Cover and simmer for about 10 minutes until soft.

Mix the cornflour with the 50ml/2fl oz water to a smooth paste and stir into the rhubarb. Cover and simmer until thick and clear. Stir in the vanilla essence. Pour the mixture into a serving dish and sprinkle with the remaining sugar. Chill for 30 minutes or more. Serve with whipped cream.

Boats moored alongside the Nyhaun in Copenhagen.

RICE AND ALMOND PUDDING
RIS AL MANDE

SERVES 8–10

900ml/1½pt milk

50g/2oz caster sugar

200g/7oz long grain white rice

50g/2oz blanched almonds, halved

1 small wine glass of sherry

1–2 tsp vanilla essence

225ml/8fl oz double cream, chilled

In the early 1800s rice was imported so it was very expensive and reserved for special occasions only. Served hot or cold, tradition demands that a bowl is put out for Father Christmas on Christmas Eve.

Bring the milk to the boil. Add the sugar and rice, stirring occasionally. Lower the heat and simmer, uncovered, for about 25 minutes or until the rice is cooked. (To test, run a grain of rice between your thumb and forefinger, if there is no hard kernel in the centre then the rice is done.) Pour the rice immediately into a shallow bowl to cool it quickly.

When cool, add the almonds, sherry and vanilla essence. Whip the cream in a chilled bowl until it thickens and holds it shape. Fold in the rice mixture. Turn the pudding into a serving dish and chill before serving. A cold sherry or raspberry sauce is often served on top.

EGG CHEESE (BUTTERMILK CHEESE)
WNIJUUSTO

SERVES 4–6

4 litres/7½pt whole milk

1.5 litres/2½pt buttermilk

4 eggs, size 4 or 5, separated

1 tsp salt

½ tsp sugar

Egg cheese makes a delicious dessert when served with fresh fruit or jam. It can be served hot.

Bring the milk slowly to the boil to prevent it burning. Mix the buttermilk, egg whites, salt and sugar. Add the mixture to the hot milk and stir well. Bring the mixture back to boil. Remove from heat and leave at room temperature until the mixture curdles completely.

Using a perforated spoon, transfer the cheese curd to a sieve and leave to drain for 30 minutes. Pour the curds into a bowl, add the egg yolks and mix well.

Take a damp piece of muslin and line a cheese mould. (If you do not have a cheese mould, a lined sieve can be used.) Spoon in the cheese. Fold the edges of the cloth over the top of the cheese. Leave to drain overnight. Turn out the cheese on to a serving dish. To serve hot, place in the oven at 230°C/450°F/Gas Mark 8 and bake for 15–20 minutes until the top is brown.

EIVOR'S ORANGE CAKE
EIVORS APELSINKAKA

SERVES 4–6

150g/5oz butter

100g/4oz sugar

3 eggs

grated rind of 2 lemons

50ml/2fl oz fresh orange juice

225g/8oz plain flour, sifted with
   2 tsp baking powder

butter for greasing

breadcrumbs for coating tin

GLAZE

100g/4oz icing sugar

2 tbsp fresh orange juice

a few drops of oil and yellow
   food colouring

candied orange peel

◄ *Eivor's orange cake*

This orange cake is light and airy with a pleasant fresh flavour. Serve with coffee or tea or as a dessert accompanied by fruit salad.

Whisk the butter and sugar until smooth and pale. Add the eggs, one at a time, stirring vigorously. Mix the lemon rind and orange juice together with the flour. Grease a 23cm/9in round cake tin with the butter and sprinkle in the breadcrumbs. Pour the mixture into the tin. Place in a cold oven. Heat the oven to 170–180°C/325–350°F/Gas Mark 3–4 and bake for 1 hour. Turn out and leave to cool under the upturned tin.

Mix the icing sugar and orange juice to a smooth glaze. Add a couple of drops of oil and colour the glaze light yellow with food colouring. Spread over the cake and scatter on the orange peel.

SPONGE CAKE WITH SOURED CREAM
KERMAKKU

SERVES 6–8

150g/5oz softened butter

225g/8oz sugar

3 eggs, size 4 or 5

425g/15oz plain flour

1 tsp bicarbonate of soda

1 tsp ground cinnamon

1 tsp ground cardamom or ginger

225ml/8fl oz soured cream

1 tsp vanilla sugar

butter for greasing

breadcrumbs for coating tin

Kermakku, a feather light sponge, is made with soured cream and delicately spiced with cinnamon, cardamom or ginger.

Preheat the oven to 170°C/325°F/Gas Mark 3. Mix the butter and sugar until light and creamy. Add one egg at a time, stirring constantly. Mix all the dry ingredients together, except the vanilla sugar and breadcrumbs. Beat half of the flour mixture into the creamed mixture. Whisk in the soured cream, the rest of the flour mixture and the vanilla sugar.

Grease a 23cm/9in round cake tin with the butter and sprinkle in the breadcrumbs. Spoon in the mixture. Bake for 50 minutes. When ready, turn out onto a wire rack and leave to cool.

MOTHER MONSEN'S BISCUITS

MOTHER MONSENS KAKE

Delicious Christmas biscuits which can be prepared up to 2 weeks in advance ready for the festive season.

MAKES 24

450g/1lb butter
450g/1lb caster sugar
4 eggs, size 4 or 5
225g/8oz plain flour
5ml/1 tsp vanilla essence
25g/1oz chopped blanched
  almonds
40g/1½oz currants

Preheat the oven to 180°C/350°F/Gas Mark 4. Cream the butter and sugar in a bowl, or food use a food processor on a low speed, until light and fluffy. Beat in one egg at a time. Add the flour and vanilla essence, then mix until smooth.

Grease a 30 x 46cm/12 x 18in Swiss roll tin. Spread the mixture evenly in the tin and sprinkle the surface with the almonds and currants. Bake for 20–25 minutes until golden brown. Leave to cool in the tin. Cut into 24 squares or triangles. To store, wrap in foil or place in an airtight container in a cool place.

Mother Monsen's biscuits ▶

MAY DAY BISCUITS

TIPPALEIVAT

May Day is carnival time which starts on the eve of April 30th called Walpurgis Night. Lots of singing and balloons are used to celebrate the arrival of spring.

MAKES 20–30

2 eggs, size 4 or 5
2 tsp sugar
1 tsp salt
200ml/7fl oz milk
400g/14oz plain flour
1–2 tsp vanilla essence
300ml/8fl oz vegetable or
   coconut oil for frying
icing sugar for dusting

Gently mix the eggs and sugar together. Add all the remaining ingredients and stir until the batter is smooth. Put the batter into a piping bag fitted with a small nozzle. Heat the oil in a pan. Squeeze the batter into the pan of hot oil making a nest-like shape. Use a metal ring in the pan if possible to keep the shape better during cooking. Remove the biscuits when they are golden brown. Drain and cool on absorbent kitchen paper. When cold, dust the biscuits with icing sugar.

CARNIVAL BUNS
FASTERLAVNSBOLLER

MAKES 8–10

DOUGH

15g/½oz dry yeast
50ml/2fl oz tepid water
25g/1oz sugar
1 egg, size 4 or 5
1 egg yolk, size 4 or 5
½ tsp salt
1 tsp ground cardamom
450g/1lb butter
175ml/6fl oz milk
450g/1lb plain flour, sifted

FILLING

100g/4oz finely chopped
   marzipan (almond paste)
2 tbsp candied mixed peel

On the Monday before Shrove Tuesday, Danish children wake up their parents early by traditionally beating them with birchwood twigs. In the afternoon they play a game called "beating a cat off the barrel" and dress up for a party afterwards when these buns are served.

Dissolve the yeast in the tepid water. Mix the sugar, egg, egg yolk, salt, cardamom and 75g/3oz of the butter. Add to the dissolved yeast. Warm the milk. Add the lukewarm milk to the mixture. Mix in the flour and the rest of the butter. Knead the dough until smooth and pliable. Add the marzipan and mixed peel. Chill for 10 minutes.

Roll out the chilled dough to 8mm/¼in thickness. Cut into 5–7.5cm/2–3in squares and put onto a greased baking tray.

Leave to rise until doubled in size. Preheat the oven to 220°C/425°F/Gas Mark 7. Bake for 12 minutes until golden brown. Sprinkle with sifted icing sugar.

Carnival buns ▶

NORWEGIAN WHOLEMEAL BREAD
NORSK HELKORNSBRØD

MAKES 1 LOAF AND 10 ROLLS OR 2 LOAVES

50g/20oz whole wheat kernels
500ml/18fl oz skimmed milk
50g/2oz fresh yeast
2 tbsp salt
1 tbsp oil
200g/7oz cottage cheese
1kg/2lb 2oz wholemeal flour
175–200g/6–7oz plain white
   flour
crushed wheat for coating

Anybody who has travelled in Norway must have envied the Norwegians their fine bread. Here is one example.

Soak the whole wheat kernels for about 1 hour in lukewarm water. Heat the milk to body temperature and stir the yeast smoothly into the liquid.

Add the salt, oil, cottage cheese, wholemeal flour, well drained wheat kernels and finally the white flour. Knead the dough until smooth. Leave to rise for 30 minutes.

Shape into one loaf and 10 rolls, or 2 loaves. Roll everything in crushed wheat. Place the loaf in a greased 1kg/2lb loaf tin and the rolls on a greased baking sheet and leave to rise until doubled in size. Preheat the oven to 200°C/400°F/Gas Mark 6. Bake the loaf for about 40–45 minutes. Bake the rolls at 220°C/425°F/Gas Mark 7 for about 20 minutes.

CAKE FROM JÄMTLAND
SÖNDAGSKAKA FRÅN JÄMTLAND

SERVES 4

3 eggs, size 1 or 2, separated

3 tbsp sugar

5 tbsp plain flour

grated rind of 1 lemon

300ml/½pt double cream or

   soured cream or

   200ml/7fl oz fromage frais

butter for greasing

breadcrumbs for coating tin

The sharp lemon flavour and smooth creamy texture of the cake makes a perfect contrast to the accompanying jam or fruit.

Preheat the oven to 180°C/350°F/Gas Mark 4. Whisk the egg yolks with the sugar and flour. Add the lemon rind. Whip the cream and stir it into the egg mixture. If using fromage frais just mix it in. Whisk the egg whites into peaks and fold into the mixture. Mix well but do not stir or the batter might sink. Pour the mixture into a greased and breadcrumbed 23cm/9in cake tin. Bake for 35–40 minutes. Do not open oven door during the first 25 minutes. Serve the cake freshly baked as dessert with any kind of jam, or berries and soft fruit.

ALMOND CONE CAKE
KRANSEKAKE

SERVES 6-8

500g/1lb 2oz almonds
500g/1lb 2oz icing sugar
3 egg whites

ICING

200g/7oz icing sugar
½ egg white
1 tsp white wine vinegar

A traditional delicacy for Norwegian National Day, May 17th. Almond cone cake is based on just 3 ingredients: almonds, icing sugar and egg whites. Decorate the finished cone with marzipan fruits for a special treat.

Blanch and skin the almonds, then leave to dry thoroughly. Grind to a paste. Place in a bowl and mix with the icing sugar. Add half of the egg whites (unwhipped) and work the dough well. Place the bowl over a pan of gently simmering water and stir in the remaining egg white. Stir continuously until the dough is lukewarm.

Preheat the oven to 170°C/325°F/Gas Mark 3. Grease and flour various sized ring moulds. These should graduate regularly in size. Ideal sizes are 7.5m/3in, 13cm/5in, 18cm/7in and 23cm/9in.

While the dough is still warm, spoon into a piping bag with a large nozzle and pipe into the ring moulds. Place the rings on trays with the various sizes within each other. Bake until light brown.

For the icing, sift the icing sugar and stir sufficient into the egg white with the vinegar until it forms firm peaks. Spoon into a piping bag fitted with a small piping nozzle. To assemble the cake, place the largest ring on a serving plate and decorate with a zig-zag pattern of icing. Stick on the next size ring and repeat the process until all of the rings are in position. The height of the cake will depend on the number of rings made.

*A stunning midsummer pole on the
Aland Islands of Finland.*

LEMON CAKE
CITRONKAK

SERVES 6–8

200g/7oz plain flour
90g/3½oz butter
50g/1oz caster sugar

CREAM

2 eggs
2 tbsp flour
½ tsp baking powder
grated rind of ½ lemon
caster sugar for sifting

The lemon flavour of the cream topping gives just the right balance to the plain but very light delicate texture of the cake.

Preheat the oven to 170°C/325°F/Gas mark 3. Mix the flour, butter and caster sugar to a dough. Press out the dough into a greased 23cm/9in cake tin. Let the dough settle. Bake for about 20 minutes. Meanwhile, mix together the ingredients for the cream, except the caster sugar. Pour the mixture over the cake base in the tin. Bake for a further 25 minutes. Turn out and let the cake cool. Sift the caster sugar on top and serve.

Lemon cake ►

ALMOND CAKES
MANDELBAKKELS

MAKES 16–20

100g/4oz bag of flaked almonds
butter for greasing
2 eggs
175g/6oz sugar
2–3 bitter almonds, grated
125g/4½oz plain flour
75g/3oz butter, melted

Easy to make, these mouthwatering little cakes, with a delicate almond flavour, need nothing extra. For a special occasion, soak the cakes in sherry or freshly squeezed orange juice with a little rum added, then top with whipped cream.

Preheat the oven to 200°C/400°F/Gas Mark 6. Toast the flaked almonds lightly then crumble or chop finely. Leave to cool. Grease 16–20 small cake moulds or patty tins well with soft butter and scatter them with the chopped almonds.

Whisk the eggs until frothy, add the sugar and whisk to a fluffy mixture. Mix in the grated almonds, flour and the cooled butter. Stir gently to prevent the mixture collapsing. Divide the mixture between the moulds and place on a baking sheet. Bake for 15 minutes. Turn out and leave to cool under the upturned moulds.

BROWN MUFFINS

BRUNA MUFFINS

There is nothing more tempting than freshly baked muffins with your coffee. These muffins have a character of their own and are good for freezing too.

MAKES 15–20

100g/4oz butter

200ml/7fl oz syrup

2 eggs

3 tbsp orange marmalade

3 tbsp cold strong coffee

3 tbsp almonds or hazelnuts, chopped

200g/7oz plain flour

2 tsp baking powder

1 tsp ground cinnamon

100ml/4fl oz single cream

Preheat the oven to 220°C/425°F/Gas Mark 7. Grease 12 muffin or deep patty tins. Work the butter until soft and creamy. Mix in the syrup. Stir in one egg at a time. Add the marmalade and coffee. Mix the almonds or hazelnuts with the flour, baking powder and cinnamon. Stir the flour mixture into the batter, alternating with the cream. Divide the mixture between the tins. Bake for about 10 minutes. Leave to cool under a cloth.

Brown muffins ▶

BISCUIT CAKE

ISCHOKLADKAKA

Biscuit cake, also called ice chocolate cake, is delicious and no cooking is needed.

SERVES 4–6

250g/9oz coconut butter
2 eggs
175g/6oz icing sugar, sifted
75g/3oz cocoa powder, sifted
100g/4oz rich tea biscuits, crushed
15–20 chocolate pieces (optional)

Melt the coconut butter in a saucepan and leave to cool. Line an oblong cake tin with greaseproof paper. Whisk the eggs and icing sugar until creamy. Stir the cocoa powder into the egg mixture. Add the fat and stir vigorously. Pour a thin layer of the mixture into the cake tin and place a layer of biscuits over. Keep repeating the layering, finishing with cocoa mixture. Leave to cool overnight (not in the freezer).

Remove the cake and place it on a serving dish. Decorate with chocolate pieces and serve by cutting thin slices.

VANILLA RINGS
VANILLE KRANSE

MAKES 20 RINGS

225g/8oz butter

225g/8oz sugar

1 egg, size 4 or 5

2 tsp vanilla essence

75g/3oz ground almonds

350g/12oz plain flour

Danish cookies and cakes are both rich and artistic. They deserve the place of honour on the coffee table.

Preheat the oven to 180°C/350°F/Gas Mark 4. Cream the butter and sugar in a bowl, or use a food processor on a low speed, until light and fluffy. Beat in the egg, then the vanilla essence, almonds and flour. Put the paste into a piping bag fitted with a star shaped nozzle. Pipe 5cm/2in rings on to a greased baking tray. Bake for about 8–9 minutes.

◄ *Vanilla rings*

LENT BUNS
LASKIAISPULLA

MAKES 20

500ml/18fl oz milk

2 eggs, size 4 or 5

200g/7oz sugar

50g/2oz fresh yeast

3 tsp salt

1 tbsp ground cardamom

225g/8oz butter or
   200ml/7fl oz vegetable oil

1.1kg/2¼lb plain flour

egg yolk for glazing

FILLING

300ml/½pt cream

1 tbsp sugar

HOT CHOCOLATE

1.5 litres/3pt milk

4 tbsp cocoa powder, sifted

2 tbsp sugar

A traditional Finnish Lent meal would be green pea soup, pig's trotters and these Lent Buns. All the bun ingredients should be at room temperature to shorten the rising time of the dough.

Warm the milk until it is lukewarm. Beat the eggs and sugar until creamy. Add the milk, yeast, salt and cardamom. (If oil is used instead of butter, add it now.) Beat in the flour and butter vigorously. Lots of air will help the dough to rise well. Knead the dough on a well floured board. Knead until it separates easily from your hands. Cover the dough with a cloth and leave to rise until doubled in size. Make 20 balls and place on a greased baking tray. Cover with a cloth and leave to rise in a warm place for about 30 minutes. Preheated oven to 190°C/375°F/Gas Mark 5.

Brush the balls with beaten egg yolk. Bake for about 30 minutes until golden brown. Remove and leave to cool on a wire rack.

For the filling, whip the cream and sugar. Cut the buns in half and fill them with the whipped cream.

For the hot chocolate, boil the milk and add the cocoa powder and sugar, whisking vigorously. Place the buns in individual bowls and pour over the hot chocolate just before serving.

INDEX